Praying Church Study Series

An Overview of God's End-Time Plan

WES HALL

SERIES EDITOR
MIKE BICKLE

International House of Prayer University

An Overview of God's End-Time Plan
by Wes Hall
Series Editor: Mike Bickle
Contributing Editors: Sam Cerny, Ian Barker, Erica Grimaldi, and Stephen Venable

Published by IHOPU Press
a division of Forerunner Publishing
International House of Prayer
3535 E. Red Bridge Road
Kansas City, MO 64137

ihopupress@ihop.org
IHOP.org
MikeBickle.org

Forerunner Publishing is the book-publishing division of the International House of Prayer of Kansas City, an evangelical missions organization that is committed to praying for the release of the fullness of God's power and purpose as we actively win the lost, heal the sick, feed the poor, make disciples, and impact society.

Printed in the United States of America

ISBN: 978-0-9823262-7-5

Cover Design: dcdstudio.com
Interior Design: Ian Barker and Dale Jimmo

Printed in the United States of America

Table of Contents

Introduction to the *Praying Church Study Series*

Welcome to *An Overview of God's End-Time Plan*! This is the second study manual in the *Praying Church Study Series*, which is based on the curriculum taught in the first semester at International House of Prayer University (IHOPU) in Kansas City. This study manual is designed to lay a broad biblical foundation for sustaining personal and corporate prayer.

Over the past several decades, the Lord has been establishing prayer ministries across the earth, some of which function twenty-four hours a day, seven days a week. One of the purposes of these ministries is to serve as a catalyst to inspire prayer in the Body of Christ. The Lord's plan is to restore a prayer culture in the Church worldwide so that the entire Church becomes a praying people—*a praying church.* This distinction is not limited to a few, but intended for everyone, just as we are called to be the healing church, the evangelizing church, and the discipling church—and all unto the renown of Jesus in the earth. Although not everyone is called to establish night-and-day prayer in their region, every believer and every community of believers is called to fervent, persevering prayer.

Jesus is the One we worship, and yet through the mystery of the Incarnation He is also our paramount teacher and premier example for our pattern of life (Matt. 23:8; 1 Pet. 2:21; 1 John 2:6). Hebrews 7:25 tells us that Jesus ever lives to make intercession. In the gospel of Luke alone, Jesus is depicted as being in the posture of prayer twelve times. Christ commands us to keep on asking, seeking, and knocking, promising that our persistence will be richly rewarded (Matt. 7:7–11; Luke 11:9–13; 18:1–8). He enjoins us to watch and pray always (Mark 13:33; Luke 21:36). And then, we find the almost limitless possibility of supplication from the lips of Jesus, beckoning us to ask anything in His name, and that the smallest faith in prayer can move mountains (Matt. 17:20; 18:19; John 14:14; 16:23). The heartbeat of the communal life of the early church was the act of prayer (Acts 1:14; 12:5). Paul was in constant prayer for the churches (Col. 1:3, 9; 1 Thess. 1:2, 3:9–10); he instructs us to be "devoted to prayer" (Rom. 12:12) and to "pray without ceasing" (1 Thess. 5:17; cf. Eph. 6:18; Col. 4:2). Peter says to be "serious and watchful in your prayers" (1 Pet. 4:7).

Why this radical emphasis on prayer in Scripture? How does one begin to obey such commands? Prayer does not occur in a vacuum, and it is not meant to be devoid of emotion and relationship. Prayer is speaking to a Person, and as those made in His image, we were created for intimate relationship with Him. Faithfulness in prayer is found by deeply knowing the character of the One before whom we stand and to whom we lift our voice.

Contrary to how God is often depicted, He is not a stoic being passively existing in a faraway realm. He is the wise, loving, and just King of the heavens and the earth—*and He has a plan which He is passionate about.* He created all things with a purpose and He will finish what He started. For prayer to be sustained, we must not only know the truth of who He is but the story He is telling. For we are, of course, praying *for something*, and that something must be informed by the Bible or we are not praying according to His will. For prayer to be ardent and ongoing, generalities will not do. We are crying, pleading, and yearning for Jesus to fulfill His plan and His purpose on earth, even as it is in heaven. The clearer we see Him, and the better we understand what He has revealed, the stronger our discipline and desire will be in the ministry of prayer. Without this vision, we will cast off restraint (Prov. 29:18) and discover neither the power nor the privilege of intercession.

The *Praying Church Study Series* begins to help us understand God's plan for His creation and the role of the Church in partnering with the Lord in prayer to see that plan executed. Our hope is that individuals and groups alike will be inspired and equipped to engage in prayer by the teachings in this series—whether it be personal or corporate prayer. Whether your primary calling is in the marketplace, the home, or full-time ministry, the principles taught in this series will be relevant as you seek to respond to the Lord's invitation.

OVERVIEW OF THE SERIES

Part 1: Understanding God's Grand Plan

This series starts with three study manuals that focus on understanding God's glorious plan to redeem the earth. We look at the present condition of the earth and study God's plan to redeem His creation and establish His kingdom on the earth in fullness. We consider the final execution of His plan in the end times and the crucial role of the praying church in partnering with God's end-time activity.

Part 2: Understanding Intercession

These three study manuals focus on the glory and practice of intercession. We examine why God governs His universe through prayer, the basic theological foundations for corporate prayer, and some biblical and historical examples of night-and-day prayer. Our aim is to be empowered to contend for a historic breakthrough of God's Spirit in the present while being strengthened to persevere in prayer for the establishing of God's kingdom in fullness on the earth at the return of Jesus.

Part 3: Foundations for Friendship with God

Just as the engine of an automobile is dependent on gasoline, so the engine of intercession requires fuel to sustain it over the long haul. The fuel for effective intercession is intimate friendship with God—why would you spend hours with someone you do not know or like, asking for things you are not sure He wants to give? The foundation for friendship with God is a right understanding of who He is and who we are to Him. Part 3 of this series explores what the Bible says about who God is, what He is really like, and the depth of His affection for His people. As we grow in the knowledge of God, we find that He empowers and sustains us in the place of fervent prayer.

Part 4: *Foundations for the Forerunner Ministry*

In the final part of this series, we discuss the forerunner ministry. The function of the priest in the Old Testament was to minister to God on behalf of men and to minister to men on behalf of God. In the same way, God is looking for a praying people who will minister to Him in unceasing prayer and prepare for the unique dynamics of the end times. Just as God used John the Baptist as a forerunner to prepare the way for Jesus' first coming, so the Lord is raising up forerunners who will boldly and fearlessly proclaim His return. In the final three manuals we look at biblical models of the forerunner ministry and the lifestyle that Jesus described in the Sermon on the Mount.

FORMAT OF THE STUDY MANUALS

Each study manual may be used for individual or group study. Each lesson includes questions and Bible references for review, discussion, and further study. In addition, suggested resources for focused and in-depth reading are provided at the end of each lesson. Many of these can be obtained through the International House of Prayer's online bookstore at IHOP.org/store, and some are available free of charge at MikeBickle.org.

The original audio and video teachings on which this series is based are hosted on IHOPU's eSchool website at IHOP.org/eschool. We encourage you to enroll in one of our many eSchool courses as a supplement to this series. Our hope is that the Lord will ignite our minds and hearts as we grow in the knowledge of God so that we would pursue the Lord with unceasing prayer!

Until He returns,

Mike Bickle,
Director, International House of Prayer

Visit IHOP.org/books/prayingchurch for further resources from the *Praying Church Study Series*.

❶ Why Should We Study the End Times?

INTRODUCTION

The generation in which the Lord returns will be the most dramatic generation in human history. The prophecies which describe this end-time generation, like those in Daniel and Revelation, are filled with images of locust-like creatures, seven-headed monsters, and seemingly mysterious numbers like the seventy "sevens" of Daniel 9 or the "666" of Revelation 13. Though some may want to dismiss these descriptions as too hard to understand, or irrelevant, they are actually meant to be understood by all. As you find your place in the great end-time drama, your heart will grow with fascination for Jesus, urgency in prayer, and confidence in God's sovereignty and good leadership. In this lesson, we will look at the importance of examining the end times, common objections to studying these prophecies, and the benefits of learning about the generation of the Lord's return.

TEACHING

I. **Studying the End Times is Foundational to the Forerunner Ministry**

   A. What is the forerunner ministry? It is the ministry of declaring in advance what the Lord is about to do on the earth before the return of Jesus, and preparing the way before Him. This is not just to relay information, but to impart confidence and love in the hearts of those who will live through the end times.

   B. Some have prayed, "Your kingdom come, Your will be done on earth as it is in heaven" (Matt. 6:10), and have hoped simply for more blessing, healing, financial provision, etc. This is not wrong, but at the same time, many negative things will happen on earth in answer to this prayer. Some will say to themselves, "This is not what I prayed for," and become offended at God and frightened by the events transpiring around them. In the face of fear and offense, forerunners are called to stand confidently in the leadership of Jesus and usher others into the same assurance.

C. Having a right understanding of the plan and purpose of God in the end times is, therefore, critical to the forerunner ministry and an essential foundation for the praying church. Paul prayed for the Colossians that they would be filled with the knowledge of God's will in all wisdom and spiritual understanding.

> *For this reason we also, since the day we heard it, do not cease to pray for you, and to ask that you may be <u>filled with the knowledge of His will in all wisdom and spiritual understanding</u>; ¹⁰that you may walk worthy of the Lord, fully pleasing Him, being fruitful in every good work and increasing in the knowledge of God; ¹¹strengthened with all might, according to His glorious power, for all patience and longsuffering with joy. (Col. 1:9–11)*

D. Understanding God's will includes having a correct (spiritual and biblical) understanding of His ways, His judgments, and His wisdom.

1. God's ways: An understanding of *what* God is doing in human history to bring everything under the leadership of His Son.

2. God's judgments: The details of *how* God will act in order to orchestrate His plan. All of God's decisions are based on His perfect justice.

3. God's wisdom: An understanding of *why* God acts the way He does. This includes understanding the wisdom of how He orchestrates history so as to bring the maximum number of human hearts into the fullness of love for Him, with the least amount of suffering, and without violating human freewill.

> *Wisdom is the principal thing; therefore get wisdom. And in all your getting, get understanding. (Prov. 4:7)*

E. If we want to understand who Jesus is and what burns on His heart, it is essential that we study the end times, since these events comprise the heart of the grand story of world redemption. The Bible is eschatological¹ by nature, for it is heading towards a goal. Without understanding the end times,

---

1   *Eschatology* is from the Greek *eschatos* meaning, "last," and *ology* meaning, "the study of." It is a branch of theology concerned with the times of the end of this age and the ultimate destiny of humanity.

we comprehend neither the overall story nor our role as the Church, walking in victory.

F. The generation in which the Lord returns is the most referenced generation in Scripture. Jesus spoke in more detail about the last generation of human history than the generation in which He lived. Why? He wanted to prepare the Bride to be victorious in love during the most dramatic time in world history. We must study the end times because the generation in which Jesus returns will manifest His heart and leadership to the nations at an unprecedented level.

G. The four gospels give us a record of Jesus' heart and power at His first coming, when He accomplished redemption on the cross. In a similar way, the end times and Jesus' return reveal His heart and power as He takes over the leadership of the whole earth.

> **The _Revelation of Jesus Christ_, which God gave Him to show His servants. (Rev. 1:1)**

H. We must study the end times because God has taken great care to announce the events of this time period through the prophets of old and by foretelling signs that will appear at the end of the age. These signs will increase in intensity as we approach the return of Jesus. God calls it wisdom to understand and discern these things because it will be an issue of life and death for people living in that hour.

> **Here is _wisdom_. Let him who has _understanding_ calculate the number of the Beast. (Rev. 13:18)**

> **Here is _the mind which has wisdom_: the seven heads are seven mountains on which the woman sits. (Rev. 17:9)**

I. The subject of eschatology is one of the most discussed subjects in Scripture (about 150 chapters discuss the generation of the Lord's return as their primary theme), yet it is one of the least understood subjects in the Body of Christ in the modern era.

II. Common Objections to Studying the End Times

A. Irrelevance

1. The first common objection is that end-time prophecy is not relevant, but only for the curious. This is often a reaction to the popular teaching that most of the end-time events take place *after* the Church has been raptured[2] (removed) from the earth.

2. In reality, the Bible clearly teaches that the Church will go through the Great Tribulation in victory and power. This differs from the pretribulation rapture view that teaches that the Church will be raptured at any minute and will miss the great end-time revival and crisis. If the pretribulation rapture were true, then almost all end-time Scripture would be irrelevant to our lives today.

3. Understanding that the Church will go through the Great Tribulation—the greatest time of pressure and crisis to ever come upon the earth—dramatically alters the significance and relevance of the end-time scriptures. Why would the Bible give us so much information about a subject that is not important to our lives in this age?

4. How we live is determined by our theology (what we believe about God). Many of God's people are not preparing adequately for the coming storm because they have a wrong theology about the end times. They erroneously assume that if the Church will not be here during that time, then what is the point of studying it?

5. Gaining understanding about the end times is a key to preparing the Church to be victorious in the most extreme glory and pressure in history. It provides us with a compass in the storm. Having understanding about the end times will be an issue of life or death to many in that hour.

B. Difficult to Understand

1. The second objection to studying the end times is that this information cannot be understood by ordinary

---

2   The word *rapture* comes from a Latin word *raptus*, and means to "catch up" or "snatch away" (Greek: *harpazo*). It is what happens to all the saints at the time of the second coming of Jesus when they are instantly changed by receiving resurrected bodies (1 Thess. 2:19; 4:17; 5:10; 2 Thess. 2:1).

believers, and is mostly symbolic, allowing only Bible scholars to understand the symbols. Furthermore, if no one can know the day or hour of Jesus' return, why give it any thought? (Matt. 24:36)

2. In truth, the scriptures on the end times were written to be understood by all of God's people. The majority of people throughout history have been uneducated peasants. Why would God put more information in His Word about the final generation than any other generation if it could not be understood by most people?

3. The Bible is not to be interpreted as mostly symbolic, but literally—at face value. It means what it says and says what it means. A good rule of thumb in Bible interpretation is this: if the plain sense makes sense, seek no other sense. Understanding that it is to be taken at face value unlocks the mysteries in a powerful way. The events and numbers in Daniel, Revelation, and other prophetic passages are to be understood in their plain, literal meaning unless it is specifically indicated that they are symbolic (Rev. 1:20; 5:6; 11:8; 12:1, 3, 9; 17:7, 9). In such cases, the context of the passage usually explains the symbols.

4. Moreover, Scripture requires those alive in the generation of the Lord's return to know the prophetic signs and to respond appropriately. Jesus and Paul emphasized the possibility of actually knowing the prophetic signs of the end times (2 Thess. 2:1–11).

Now learn this parable from the fig tree: when its branch has already become tender and puts forth leaves, you know that summer is near. ³³So you also, <u>when you see all these things, know that it is near</u>—at the doors! (Matt. 24:32–33)

There will be signs in the sun, in the moon, and in the stars; and on the earth distress of nations, with perplexity, the sea and the waves roaring; ²⁶men's hearts failing them from fear and the expectation of those things which are coming on the earth, for the powers of the heavens will be shaken. ²⁷Then they will see the Son of Man coming in a cloud with power and great glory. ²⁸Now <u>when these things begin to happen, look up</u>

[have a heavenly perspective] and <u>lift up your heads</u> [be encouraged in faith], because your redemption draws near. (Luke 21:25–28)

Concerning the times and the seasons, brethren, you have no need that I should write to you. ²For <u>you yourselves know perfectly</u> that the day of the Lord so comes as a thief in the night. . . . ⁴But <u>you, brethren, are not in darkness, so that this Day should overtake you as a thief</u>. . . . ⁵You are all sons of light and sons of the day. . . . ⁶Therefore . . . <u>let us watch</u>. (1 Thess. 5:1–2, 4–6)

5. As we grasp the basic truths of the end times, we have confidence and zeal to go deeper in our study of other end-time passages. One of the biggest hindrances today is the conclusion that end-time prophecy is too difficult to understand, leading many to ask, "Why even try?" In actuality, these prophecies are for all of us to comprehend.

III. Five Benefits of Studying the End Times

Those who do wickedly against the covenant he shall corrupt with flattery; but the people who know their God shall be strong, and carry out great exploits. ³³And those of the people who understand shall instruct many. (Dan. 11:32–33)

A. Benefit #1: We will have confidence in the hour of trial.

1. The Bible tells us that before Jesus returns there will be a great falling away from the faith (2 Thess. 2:3). The love of many will grow cold because of great deception, a love for wickedness, and offense at the leadership of Jesus (Matt. 24:11–12). People will be persuaded to choose sin over righteousness because they will not understand the hour in which they are living and will be offended by God's activity. Scripture is clear that those who fall away will have the same fate as that of unbelievers—eternal separation from God.

2. The knowledge of who Jesus is, what He is like, and how He acts will keep us steady in the hour of trouble that is coming upon the earth when God shakes everything that can be shaken (Heb. 12:26). Conversely, not understanding

God's ways will cause our hearts to draw back in offense and anger at God as the events of the end times unfold.

3. Paul understood that staying steady until Jesus' return would require two things: patience and endurance (Col. 1:11). We need patience because of the delay preceding Jesus' return (it is going to take time). We need endurance because great trouble is in store for believers in the days ahead (it is going to involve pain).

4. Jesus Himself addressed these two issues at His first coming. He knew that many would not stay steady in prayer until the end, and warned that men would faint from fear of what was coming upon the earth.

   And shall God not avenge _His own elect who cry out day and night to Him, though He bears long with them?_ _⁸I tell you that He will avenge them speedily. Nevertheless, when the Son of Man comes, will He really find faith_ _on the earth? (Luke 18:7–8)_

   . . . men's hearts failing them from fear and the expectation of those things which are coming on the earth. (Luke 21:26)

5. Paul outlines four main ways in which believers benefit from being a man or woman of understanding (Col. 1:9–11).

   a. *A life that fully pleases God* by not drawing back in compromise or fear, but by walking in full obedience and holiness.

   b. *A fruitful ministry* that blossoms from the place of fervent prayer and of doing great exploits for God.

   c. *Growing in the knowledge of God* by being fascinated with God instead of being offended by Him.

   d. *Supernatural strength to persevere* in times of trial through the cultivation of patience and endurance.

6. Studying the end times gives us an understanding that the Church will be victorious in the end. This motivates us to press in and not draw back, confident in God's sovereign rule. We will be at peace in the midst of the storm, and

this peace will lead to right decisions and the courage to pursue God.

B. Benefit #2: We will become a people of understanding who prepare others.

1. God is going to establish a people who "know their God" and possess understanding of His plans and purposes (Dan. 11:32–33). Daniel tells us that this group will be "strong," meaning they will possess great inner strength and righteousness in the midst of fiery trials. They will not be offended with Jesus or draw back in fear. They will also do "great exploits," by being anointed with power for "greater works than these" (John 14:12). In addition, these men and women will "instruct many," by making sense of God's activity for others.

2. The prepared, prophetic Church will have the answer to keep many from being offended by God's actions in the end times. She will be able to answer the question of why a God of love would allow, and even orchestrate, the events that happen during the Great Tribulation. The purpose of God's judgments is to remove everything that hinders the revelation of God's love, so that multitudes will be saved and grow mature in love for God.

3. God is preparing messengers who are filled with a right understanding of His will, and who are able to instruct others by rightly interpreting the signs of the times. God is looking for "watchmen" who will listen, understand, and proclaim His purposes, in order to prepare people for what is coming to the earth. He is seeking those like Jeremiah, Ezekiel, Zechariah, Anna, John the Baptist, and John the Apostle who "ate the scroll" (Ezek. 3:1; Rev. 10:9–10) of God's word, and who were altogether consumed with the purposes of God.

    Son of man, I have made you a watchman for the house of Israel; therefore hear a word from My mouth, and give them warning from Me. (Ezek. 3:17)

4. God is looking for a people in these days who, like the sons of Issachar in King David's day, have an understanding of the times and seasons of God's activity, and know how

to live on the earth as the people of God. Such a people will not be taken aback or offended with God's ways, because they have taken time to gain a spirit of wisdom and understanding concerning His purposes.

> *Of the sons of Issachar who had understanding of the times, to know what Israel ought to do, their chiefs were two hundred; and all their brethren were at their command. (1 Chr. 12:32)*

5. God is preparing "Day of the Lord" preachers (those with understanding of the coming crisis like Noah and John the Baptist) to prepare people for the coming of the Lord. These people must have an understanding of the end times.

> *Blow the trumpet in Zion, and sound an alarm in My holy mountain! Let all the inhabitants of the land tremble; for the day of the LORD is coming, for it is at hand. (Joel 2:1)*

C. Benefit #3: We will become urgent in intercession.

An understanding of the end-time scriptures will give us a sense of urgency to live a life of prayer and cultivate greater spiritual depth. Furthermore, we will grow in faith that our prayers can release, stop, and minimize God's judgments, while increasing His glory, in specific geographic areas. Our prayers can change history by leading many to salvation and protection (Exod. 32:9–14; Joel 2:12–19).

D. Benefit #4: We will understand the continuity of our labors.

Understanding the end times causes us to see the continuity between what we do now, and how we will be rewarded in the age to come. This life can be likened to a "seventy-year internship" that prepares us for our primary assignment of ruling with Jesus in the age to come. One of the main reasons we are often weighed down with the cares of this life rather than living in light of eternity is because we have not adequately given ourselves to studying our eternal destiny.

E. Benefit #5: We will become fascinated with Jesus.

Studying the end times causes us to be fascinated with Jesus, because it is the study of His glory, His leadership, and

His ways. The more we study His ways, the more we fall in love with Him. Many believers lack understanding of the end times, so their spirits are not fascinated with the beauty of His leadership.

IV. Becoming a People of Spiritual Understanding

A. God has given weak and broken human beings the ability and the glory of knowing His mysteries, His will, and the secrets of His heart. It is essential that the end-time church be familiar with what God says about the time of His return.

It is the glory of God to conceal a matter, but <u>the glory of kings is to search out a matter</u>. (Prov. 25:2)

That <u>you may prove</u> what the will of God is, that which is good and acceptable and perfect. (Rom. 12:2, NASB)

B. Daniel tells us that in the end times God is going to release understanding of His plans and purposes to those who are wise.

Many shall be purified, made white, and refined, but the wicked shall do wickedly; and none of the wicked shall understand, but <u>the wise shall understand</u>. (Dan. 12:10)

C. What is God's pathway to wisdom and understanding? It involves a twofold process of diligent preparation by the believer and the sovereign impartation of God's Spirit. We enter into this true understanding primarily through prayerful study of God's Word. Daniel 9:2–3 gives us great insight into this process, explaining how Daniel received one of the greatest revelations of God's end-time purpose for Israel and the nations (9:22).

1. Daniel "understood by the books" (9:2), meaning he earnestly studied God's Word.

2. Daniel lived a lifestyle of "prayer and supplications, with fasting" (9:3).

D. Study of the end times is not, as many assume, about intellectual exercise and a debating spirit. It is important that we do not get into argumentative debates with those who think differently, but that we disagree in love and meekness. A destructive, debating spirit arises if we are studying the end times purely as an academic exercise. A correct understanding of the end times should produce a people who give themselves to fervent prayer, a holy lifestyle according to the Sermon on the Mount, and prophetic proclamation of the gospel of the kingdom. We should study diligently in order to apply these truths to our lives now.

SUMMARY

If you knew that your journey would be an easy one, like a stroll through the park on a warm, sunny day, what items would you take with you? On the other hand, if you knew that your journey would be difficult—through mountains, valleys, and stormy weather—what would you put in your backpack? What we know about the journey ahead will affect how we pack and prepare for it. In the same way, what we know about the end times will determine how we prepare for those days. Thus, having correct eschatology is not just a side issue or a fringe topic, but vital to our Christian lives here and now.

QUESTIONS

Reviewing (see answers on page 97)

A. The subject of eschatology is the most _____ subject in Scripture, yet it is the least _____ subject in the Bible.

B. Which of the following is true:
    1. The Church will be raptured before the Great Tribulation.
    2. The Church will go through the Great Tribulation.
    3. The Great Tribulation represents trials experienced throughout church history.
    4. The Church will be raptured at the abomination of desolation.

C. True or False: Unless the Bible says it is symbolic, it means what it says and says what it means.

D. Not understanding God's ways will cause our hearts to draw back in _____ and _____ at God as the events of the end times unfold.

E. Studying the end times causes us to be fascinated with Jesus because it is a study of His _____, His _____, and His _____.

Small Group Discussion

A. Why is it true that if we do not understand the end times, we will not understand the overall story of Scripture (Dan. 11:32–33; Amos 3:7–8; Matt. 24:32–33; Col. 1:9–11; Rev. 1:1)?

B. How do we begin to answer the question of why a God of love would allow and even orchestrate the events in the Great Tribulation (Isa. 26:9; Jer. 9:24; Eph. 1:17–19; Jas. 4:8; Rev. 19:2)?

C. God said that many would grow weary in the place of prayer and that men's hearts would fail them for fear as the tribulation events unfold (Matt. 24:9–12; Luke 21:25–28; 2 Thess. 2:3). How can you cultivate faithfulness in the place of prayer to prepare yourself and others for that hour (Ps. 27:4; Prov. 25:2; Isa. 40:31; Ezek. 3:17; Matt. 25:1–13; Gal. 6:7–9)?

D. This lesson discussed the great falling away from the faith (Matt. 24:12; 2 Thess. 2:3). Does that mean that believers can lose their salvation? What evidence in the Bible leads to this conclusion (Matt. 24:13; Phil. 2:12; 2 Pet. 3:17; Rev. 3:5)?

E. Daniel received more revelation about the end times than almost any other person (Dan. 7:1–12:13). What parts of Daniel's life can you imitate in your own life (Dan. 1:8; 2:17–18; 5:14; 6:10; 9:2–3)? What practical steps can you take to follow his example (Pss. 1:2; 132:2–5; Matt. 5:3–7:27; Eph. 6:10–19; Jude 20)?

FURTHER RESOURCES

Books

Ladd, George Eldon. *The Blessed Hope: A Biblical Study of the Second Advent and the Rapture.* Grand Rapids, MI: Wm. B. Eerdmans, 1990.

Lockyer, Herbert. *All About the Second Coming.* Peabody, MA: Hendrickson, 1998.

Sliker, David. *End Times Simplified.* Kansas City, MO: Forerunner Books, 2005.

Articles

Various. *100 Most Frequently Asked Questions about the End Times.* http://www.MikeBickle.org.

———. *150 Chapters on the End Times.* http://www.MikeBickle.org.

———. *Glossary of End-Time Terms.* http://www.MikeBickle.org.

Audio

Bickle, Mike. *The Coming Eschatological Revolution Part 1*. December 28, 2008. http://www.MikeBickle.org.

——. *The Coming Eschatological Revolution Part 2*. December 29, 2008. http://www.MikeBickle.org.

——. *God's End-Time Prophetic Plan: 3 Essential Parts*. April 3, 2005. http://www.MikeBickle.org.

——. *Introducing the Second Coming Procession*. September 3, 2005. http://www.MikeBickle.org.

——. *Jesus' Procession across the Sky to Rapture the Church*. September 17, 2005. http://www.MikeBickle.org.

——. *Overview of the Main People and Events in the End Times*. July 31, 2009. http://www.MikeBickle.org.

❷ Can We Know the Generation of the Lord's Return?

INTRODUCTION

Prophetic signs serve the Church in the same way a weather station serves a geographic region. In weather stations, meteorologists track the weather patterns and forecast when severe weather is approaching. For instance, they can identify stormy conditions that are likely to produce tornados. When that happens, tornado sirens sound a warning throughout the affected cities or towns. While meteorologists may not know the precise moment or spot on which a tornado will touch down, they can track the conditions suitable for those twisters and alert the people in the region. The prophetic signs of the end times are like these early warning systems, and, if discerned, people can be prepared for what is coming. In essence, though we cannot know the day or the hour of the Lord's return, we can know when we are in the generation of His return based on the observation of clear, biblical signs. In this lesson, we will look at essential, biblical truths concerning the unique aspects of the generation of the Lord's return so we can become confident in discerning the signs of the times.

TEACHING

I. **We Can and Should Recognize the Generation of the Lord's Return**

   A. The subject of the signs of the times is greatly neglected by the Body of Christ, yet many scriptures emphasize how important prophetic signs are at the end of the age. Scripture shows that Jesus, more than any of the apostles, taught on our need to discern the times. He gave severe rebukes to those who did not pay attention to the prophetic signs that pointed to His first coming (Matt. 16:1–4; Luke 19:42–44). Jesus also mandated that we pay attention to the signs marking His return (Matt. 24:32–44; Luke 21:34–36).

   B. Scripture gives many specific and detailed signs that identify the final generation as unique in history. However, much of the Church is unfamiliar with these signs and wrongly assumes that because Jesus told His disciples that no one knows the day or the hour of His return (Matt. 24:36; 25:13), we should therefore be unconcerned and not watch for it.

C. It is clear from Scripture that we cannot know the day or the hour of Jesus' return, and thus we should not seek to engage in the practice of predicting dates and times for this event. Nevertheless, we need to clearly answer the question, "Can and should we know the generation of the Lord's return, and, if yes, what are the signs of His coming?" It is possible to know the generation in which the Lord returns, and God promised to give prophetic signs so that people can make the necessary preparations for what is coming.

D. It is the opinion of some on the leadership team at the International House of Prayer of Kansas City, that though we do not and cannot know the day or the hour, it is possible that Jesus could return within the lifetime of people alive today. This opinion is based on study and observation of the biblical signs of the times as recorded in the teaching of Scripture, rather than on any kind of personal or special revelation.

E. Knowing the times is critical, and Jesus rebuked the leaders of Israel for being unable to read the prophetic signs at His first coming. They came under judgment for being unresponsive to God because they did not know the time of their His visitation.

He answered and said to them, "When it is evening you say, 'It will be fair weather, for the sky is red'; ³and in the morning, 'It will be foul weather today, for the sky is red and threatening.' <u>Hypocrites! You know how to discern the face of the sky, but you cannot discern the signs of the times</u>." (Matt. 16:2–3)

For days will come upon you when your enemies will . . . ⁴⁴level you, and your children within you, to the ground; . . . because you did not <u>know</u> the <u>time of your visitation</u>. (Luke 19:43–44)

F. It is common for people to misuse Jesus' statement in the Olivet Discourse (Matt. 24:36; Mark 13:32) to justify their lack of study on the end times, their unfamiliarity with biblical prophecy, and their lethargy in preparing for His return. They wrongly conclude that no one can ever know the time-frame of the

Lord's return, and, in light of this, they do nothing to prepare themselves or others for that hour of history.

G. This attitude is reflected in the common statement about eschatology, "I am neither 'premill' nor 'postmill'. I am 'pan-mill'; it will all pan out in the end." Yes, it will all pan out in the end, but that is not the real question. The real question is, "Will it pan out well for you?" Will you be prepared, and will you have prepared others? This is the point that Jesus makes in the following passage:

> But *of that day and hour no one knows*, not even the angels of heaven, but My Father only. ³⁷*But as the days of Noah were, so also will the coming of the Son of Man be.* ³⁸*For as in the days before the flood, they were eating and drinking, marrying and giving in marriage, until the day that Noah entered the ark,* ³⁹*and did not know until the flood came and took them all away, so also will the coming of the Son of Man be.* ⁴⁰*Then two men will be in the field: one will be taken and the other left.* ⁴¹*Two women will be grinding at the mill: one will be taken and the other left.* ⁴²*Watch therefore, for you do not know what hour your Lord is coming.* ⁴³*But know this, that if the master of the house had known what hour the thief would come, he would have watched and not allowed his house to be broken into.* ⁴⁴*Therefore you also be ready, for the Son of Man is coming at an hour you do not expect.* (Matt. 24:36–44)

H. Jesus explained that no one but the Father knows the day and the hour (Matt. 24:36), but He didn't say that we could not know the season or the conditions surrounding His second coming. In the verses preceding and following this teaching, Jesus exhorted His disciples to be watchful and to know the season, which means to be familiar with the conditions surrounding His coming.

> Now learn this parable from the fig tree: When its branch has already become tender and puts forth leaves, you know that summer is near. ³³*So you also, when you see all these things [the signs about which He has spoken earlier], know that it is near—at the doors!* ³⁴*Assuredly, I say to you, this generation will by no means pass away till all these things*

take place. ³⁵Heaven and earth will pass away, but My words will by no means pass away. (Matt. 24:32–35)

<u>Watch therefore</u>, for you know neither the day nor the hour in which the Son of Man is coming. (Matt. 25:13)

I.   Furthermore, Scripture tells us that the Lord does nothing without first announcing it through His servants, the prophets. How much more can we expect the Lord to announce the return of His Son to the earth?

Surely <u>the Lord GOD does nothing, unless He reveals His secret to His servants the prophets</u>. ⁸A lion has roared! Who will not fear? The Lord GOD has spoken! Who can but prophesy? (Amos 3:7–8)

J.   Consider this example given by Jesus. In Noah's day, the flood came both suddenly and unexpectedly upon those who were unprepared and ignorant of the hour in which they lived. Yet God had announced this coming cataclysmic judgment generations beforehand through Enoch and Methuselah.³ God also provided a major sign of the flood when He instructed Noah to start building an ark over a hundred years before the rains came.

<u>Enoch lived sixty-five years, and begot Methuselah.</u> ²²After he begot Methuselah, Enoch walked with God three hundred years, and had sons and daughters. ²³So all the days of Enoch were three hundred and sixty-five years. ²⁴And Enoch walked with God; and he was not, for God took him. (Gen. 5:21–24)

---

3   The exact meaning of "Methuselah" is somewhat uncertain. Dr. Henry Morris said it may mean, *"When he dies, judgment."* Stelman Smith and Judson Corn-wall in their work, *Exhaustive Dictionary of Bible Names,* (FL: Bridge-Logos, 1998), interpreted "Methuselah" as, *"When he is dead it shall be sent,"* with the "it" referring to the deluge. One thing that is clear from the Bible is that Methuselah is the oldest man of whom we have any record. This very ancient man lived before the flood and died at the age of 969 years, in the year of the flood (Gen. 5:21–27; 1 Chr. 1:3). This fact, plus the former possible meaning of his name, suggests that Methuselah's very godly father, Enoch, received a prophecy from God when his son was born, thus the name. Methuselah's great age may be further evidence of God's longsuffering in the days of Noah (1 Pet. 3:20; 2 Pet. 3:9). "Methuselah—WebBible Encyclopedia," ChristianAnswers. net, accessed November 22, 2010, http://christiananswers.net/dictionary/ methuselah.html.

K. Noah and his family were not taken by surprise. Noah clearly understood the signs of the times in his generation and made preparations accordingly. Furthermore, God explicitly told Noah that the rain would come in "seven more days" (Gen. 7:4). His great-grandfather, Enoch, prophesied God's coming judgment (Jude 14–15) and he knew that when his grandfather Methuselah died, judgment would come.

> *And the LORD said, "My Spirit shall not strive with man forever, for he is indeed flesh; yet his days shall be one hundred and twenty years." (Gen. 6:3)*

> *God said to Noah, "The end of all flesh has come before Me, for the earth is filled with violence through them; and behold, I will destroy them with the earth. . . . ^{7:4}For <u>after seven more days</u> I will cause it to rain on the earth forty days and forty nights, and I will destroy from the face of the earth all living things that I have made." (Gen. 6:13; 7:4)*

> *By faith Noah, being <u>divinely warned</u> of things not yet seen, <u>moved with godly fear, prepared</u> an ark for the saving of his household, <u>by which</u> he <u>condemned the world</u> and became heir of the righteousness which is according to faith. (Heb. 11:7)*

L. Paul also taught that the Church should know the times and seasons related to the Lord's coming.

> *Concerning the <u>times and the seasons</u>, brethren, you have <u>no need</u> that I should write to you. ²For you yourselves know perfectly that the day of the Lord so comes as a thief in the night [the unprepared suffer unnecessary loss]. . . . ⁴<u>But you, brethren, are not in darkness</u>, so that this Day should <u>overtake</u> you as a thief. . . . ⁶<u>Therefore</u> . . . let <u>us watch and be sober</u>. (1 Thess. 5:1–2, 4–6)*

II. The Eschatological Nature of Scripture

A. The generation of the Lord's return, along with the generation of His first coming, are described more than any other generation in Scripture. Eighty-nine chapters in the Gospels, not to mention numerous details given to us in the epistles, document the first coming of Jesus, while over 150 chapters address the subject of the end times and the second coming.[4]

B.   Shortly after the birth of the Church, Peter declared that the main theme of Scripture was the return of Jesus and the restoration of all things. He said that all the Old Testament prophets prophesied mainly about two generations:

1.   The first generation was the one in which Jesus would suffer and rise from the dead.

But those things which God foretold by the mouth of all His prophets, that the Christ would suffer, He has thus fulfilled. (Acts 3:18)

2.   The second generation is the one in which Jesus will return. All of God's prophets since the world began have foretold "the times of restoration of all things" when a generation would witness the return of Jesus.

Repent therefore and be converted, that your sins may be blotted out, so that times of refreshing may come from the presence of the Lord, ²⁰and that He may send Jesus Christ, who was preached to you before, ²¹whom heaven must receive until the <u>times of restoration of all things, which God has spoken by the mouth of all His holy prophets since the world began</u>. (Acts 3:19–21)

C.   In other words, we cannot say that we are familiar with God's heart and His will until we recognize the central importance of these themes, and begin to apply ourselves to what they say. If the theme of the final generation is so important to the Lord, it is essential that we give ourselves to studying what Scripture says about this generation, and respond appropriately.

D.   Part of our failure to understand the eschatological nature of Scripture has been that many of us were taught that the Old Testament has only historic and symbolic meaning to our lives today. However, much of the Old Testament was written with a future, or eschatological, fulfillment in view.

1.   C. E. B. Cranfield suggests that Jesus believed the historical and the eschatological were mingled, and that the final

---

4   See "150 Chapters on the End Times," Mike Bickle, accessed February 28, 2011, http://mikebickle.org/resources/resource/2888?return_url.

eschatological event is seen through the "transparency" of the immediate historical context.

In the crises of history the eschatological is foreshadowed. The divine judgments in history are, so to speak, rehearsals of the last judgment and the successive incarnations of antichrist are foreshadowings of the last supreme concentration of the rebelliousness of the devil before the End.[5]

2. George Eldon Ladd applied this thesis to the Old Testament prophets and found this foreshortened view of the future to be one of the essential elements in the prophetic perspective.

In Amos, the Day of the Lord is both an historical (Amos 5:18–20) and an eschatological event (Amos 7:4; 8:8–9; 9:5). Isaiah describes the historical day of visitation on Babylon as though it was the eschatological Day of the Lord (Isa. 13). Zephaniah describes the Day of the Lord (Zeph. 1:7, 14) as an historical disaster at the hands of an unarmed foe (Zeph. 1:10–12, 16–17; 2:5–15); but he also describes it in terms of a worldwide catastrophe in which all creatures are swept off the face of the earth (Zeph. 1:2–3) so that nothing remains (Zeph. 1:18).[6]

3. Walter Kaiser appears to hold a similar view stating that the historic fulfillments of prophecy are often no more than down payments of a future, final fulfillment at the end of the age. In other words, much of the prophetic scriptures have both a local and historical (near) fulfillment, and a global and eschatological (far) fulfillment.

Thus the promise was not simply a predictive word that remained inert and in word form only until it was fulfilled in its end point; it was a word that was maintained over the centuries in a continuing series of historic fulfillments that acted as earnests, or down payments on that word that still pointed to the last or final fulfillment.[7]

5   C. E. B. Cranfield, "St. Mark 13," *Scottish Journal of Theology* 6, no. 3 (1953): 300.
6   George Eldon Ladd and Donald A. Hagner, *Theology of the New Testament* (Grand Rapids, MI: Wm. B. Eerdmans, 1993), 198–199.
7   Walter C. Kaiser, *The Promise-Plan of God* (Grand Rapids, MI: Zondervan, 2008), 19.

There were not numerous predictions arbitrarily and randomly scattered throughout the Old Testament and then fulfilled now and again in the New Testament. . . . God used [historical events] in giving mini-fulfillments through the course of history that were an essential part of the final fulfillment but certainly not to the extent and awesomeness of the completion in space and time of the final word and fulfillment announced ages prior to its resolution.[8]

III. The Uniqueness of the Last Generation

Another parable He put forth to them, saying: "The kingdom of heaven is like a man who sowed good seed in his field; 25but while men slept, his enemy came and sowed tares among the wheat and went his way. 26But when the grain had sprouted and produced a crop, then the tares also appeared. 27So the servants of the owner came and said to him, 'Sir, did you not sow good seed in your field? How then does it have tares?' 28He said to them, 'An enemy has done this.' <u>The servants said to him, 'Do you want us then to go and gather them up?'</u> 29<u>But he said, 'No, lest while you gather up the tares you also uproot the wheat with them. 30Let both grow together until the harvest</u>, and at the time of harvest I will say to the reapers, 'First gather together the tares and bind them in bundles to burn them, but gather the wheat into my barn.'" (Matt. 13:24–30)

A. Jesus said that there would be one generation in history in which the wheat and the tares would mature together and which would culminate in a great harvest. It will be a day of great fruitfulness for the kingdom, yet it will also be a day of the fullness of sin and the fullness of Satan's rage on earth.

B. How long is a biblical generation? A generation in Scripture ranges from forty to one hundred years (Num. 32:13; Ps. 90:10; Acts 7:6; cf. Gen. 15:16). Moses spoke of Israel's captivity in Egypt as lasting four hundred years or four generations (Gen. 15:13). There were fourteen generations from Abraham to David (Matt. 1:17) each averaging about seventy years. So, we can conclude that when the Bible speaks of that final generation, it will be within the above-mentioned range of years.

---

8   Ibid., 25.

C. It is possible to identify four unique dynamics that will be present in the generation of the Lord's return that have not been present in any other generation in history. The people of God must be prepared more than ever before to navigate the challenges that will arise in the events of this period.

1. The Fullness of God's Power

   a. The generation of the Lord's return will witness the power of God in an unprecedented way. The spirit of prophecy will be poured out on the Church in fullness (Acts 2:17), as the Church walks in the power and authority of Jesus (John 14:12), and witnesses the greatest harvest of souls the earth has ever seen (Rev. 7:9–17).

   b. At the same time, the praying church will partner with Jesus as He looses the temporal judgments of God against the Antichrist and his kingdom (Rev. 8:4–6). We will witness the power of the book of Acts and the book of Exodus, combined and multiplied on a global scale, before the return of Christ (Mic. 7:15).

2. The Fullness of Sin

   As the wheat comes to fullness, so do the tares. Scripture tells us that the last generation will witness the greatest demonstration of wickedness, that will be manifest in numerous ways, as the fullness of man's sin is expressed openly (Dan. 8:23; 12:10; Rev. 9:21; 14:18–19).

   But the rest of mankind, who were not killed by these plagues, did not repent of the works of their hands, that they should not worship demons, and idols . . . [21]and they did not repent of their murders or their sorceries or their sexual immorality or their thefts. (Rev 9:20–21)

   a. Lawlessness (Matt. 24:12; 2 Thess. 2:7)

   b. Sexual Immorality[9] (2 Pet. 3:3; Rev. 9:21; 17:2; 18:3; 19:2)

---

9 Every second $3,075.64 is spent on pornography worldwide; 28,258 Internet users are viewing pornography; and 372 Internet users type adult search terms into search engines. Every thirty-nine minutes a new pornographic movie is being created in the United States. In regards to the 2006 worldwide pornography revenues, $97.06 billion was spent. This means that the pornography industry is larger than the combined revenues of the top technology companies includ-

      c. Murder[10] (Dan. 7:21, 25; 8:24; 11:33–35; 12:7, 10; Mark 13:12–13; Luke 21:12, 16–17; 2 Tim. 3:3; Rev. 6:9–11; 7:13–14; 9:21; 13:7, 10; 16:6; 17:6; 18:24; 19:2)

      d. Theft (Rev. 9:21)

      e. Hatred of God (Ps. 2:1–3; Rev. 11:18; 13:5–6; 16:9, 11, 21)

      f. Declaring War on God (Dan. 7:21; Rev. 13:7; 17:14; 19:19)

      g. Relational Breakdown[11] (Matt. 24:10–12; Mark 13:9, 12–13; Luke 21:12, 16–17)

      h. Idolatry (Rev. 9:20; 13:4, 8; 14:11)

      i. Sorceries (occult and drugs) (Rev. 13:3, 12–15; 16:13–14; 18:23)

      j. Deception (Matt. 24:5, 11, 12, 24; 2 Thess. 2:3–4; 1 Tim. 4:1–3; 1 John 2:1–27)

   3. The Fullness of Deception

      a. Jesus warned that deception would be one of the enemy's primary tactics in the end times. Through false prophets, Satan will attack the truth of God's Word

---

ing Microsoft, Google, Amazon, eBay, Yahoo!, Apple, Netflix, and Earthlink. "Pornography Statistics," Family Safe Media, accessed November 17, 2010, http://familysafemedia.com/pornography_ statistics.html; "Stats on Internet Pornography," Online MBA, accessed November 29, 2010, http://www.onlinemba.com/blog/stats-on-internet-pornography/.

10 We live in one of the most violent eras of human history. It is estimated that in the twentieth century alone, deaths related to genocide and tyranny totaled eighty-three million along with forty-two million combat-related deaths. Forty-four million people died in the twentieth century due to government induced starvation and famine, and Communism alone accounted for ninety-two million deaths (statistics based on averages from "Deaths by Mass Unpleasantness: Estimated Totals for the Entire 20th Century," Historical Atlas of the Twentieth Century, accessed January 28, 2011, http://users.rcn.com/mwhite28/warstat8.htm). There have been over fifty-three million abortions performed in the United States since 1973 ("Abortion Statistics: United States Data and Trends," National Right to Life, accessed June 2, 2011, http://www.nrlc.org/Factsheets/FS03_AbortionInTheUS.pdf). In 2003, an estimated 41.6 million abortions were performed worldwide (Singh, S. et al., *Abortion Worldwide: A Decade of Uneven Progress* (New York: Guttmacher Institute, 2009), http://www.guttmacher.org/pubs/Abortion-Worldwide.pdf (accessed December 6, 2010)).

11 Beyond the current divorce rates nationally and worldwide, there is a current assault on the very definition and institution of marriage itself by homosexual activists seeking to redefine marriage, specifically as it pertains to marital benefits and privileges.

as being irrelevant, false, and even dangerous. These lies will play on the human desire to engage in compromising, sinful pleasures (Dan. 11:21; Matt. 24:11, 12, 24; 2 Thess. 2:3–4; Rev. 9:20–21; 13:3–4, 8, 12–15; 14:11; 16:13–14; 18:23).

Take heed that no one deceives you. ⁵For many will come in My name, saying, "I am the Christ," and will deceive many. (Matt. 24:4–5)

The coming of the lawless one is according to the working of Satan, with all power, signs, and lying wonders, ¹⁰and with all unrighteous deception among those who perish. (2 Thess. 2:9–10)

Now the Spirit expressly says that in latter times some will depart from the faith, giving heed to deceiving spirits and doctrines of demons. (1 Tim. 4:1)

b.   Moreover, there will also be a delusion sent by God. Many people will choose a life of compromise and sin (short-term pleasure) over righteousness, and God will give them over to what they choose (Rom. 1:24–25).

They did not receive the love of the truth, that they might be saved. ¹¹And for this reason God will send them strong delusion, that they should believe the lie, ¹²that they all may be condemned who did not believe the truth but had pleasure in unrighteousness (2 Thess. 2:10–12)

4.   The Fullness of Tribulation (Jer. 30:7; Dan. 12:1)

Jesus prophesied a time of unprecedented trouble, hardship, and suffering that would come to the earth:

Then there will be great tribulation, such as has not been since the beginning of the world until this time, no, nor ever shall be. (Matt. 24:21)

This tribulation will be a result of:

a.   Man's Sin (Pss. 2:1–3; 83:1–18; Zech. 14:1–2)

Then they will deliver you up to tribulation and kill you, and you will be hated by all nations for My name's sake. (Matt. 24:9)

b.   Satan's Rage (Dan. 7:21, 25; Rev. 12:12–13; 13:1–18)

Woe to the inhabitants of the earth . . . For the devil has come down to you, having great wrath, because he knows that he has a short time. (Rev. 12:12)

c.   God's Judgments (Isa. 63:1–6; Rev. 14:10; 15:7)

Then I saw another sign in heaven, great and marvelous: seven angels having the seven last plagues, for in them the wrath of God is complete. (Rev. 15:1)

d.   Creation's Groan—earthquakes, volcanoes, storms, and violent weather patterns (Matt. 24:29; Rom. 8:19–22)

The earth is violently broken, the earth is split open, the earth is shaken exceedingly. ²⁰The earth shall reel to and fro like a drunkard, and shall totter like a hut; its transgression shall be heavy upon it, and it will fall, and not rise again. (Isa. 24:19–20)

Whose voice then shook the earth; but now He has promised, saying, "Yet once more I shake not only the earth, but also heaven." (Heb. 12:26)

SUMMARY

We are entering days when the fullness of man's sin, the devil's deception, the world's tribulations, and God's zeal and power will be openly manifested for all to see. In this hour, it is crucial to rightly position our heart, mind, and will before God. Now, more than ever, we are to give ourselves to prayer and fasting so that we may walk in God's power; spend time in study of His Word so that we might resist Satan's deceptions; and trust Him wholeheartedly in order to endure seasons of suffering. The direction of our heart will determine the course of our life. Therefore, in these days, let the first and greatest commandment be your first and highest priority. Love God with all your heart, mind, soul, and strength.

QUESTIONS

Reviewing (see answers on page 97)

A. True or False—It is possible to know the generation in which the Lord returns.

B. Which of the following were signs for Noah's generation, telling that a cataclysmic, worldwide judgment was coming?

1. The death of Noah's grandfather, Methuselah.

2. The gradual increase of rainstorms throughout Noah's lifetime.

3. Noah's building of the ark.

4. God's word to Noah about sending rain in seven days.

C. Much of the Old Testament was written with a _____ or _____ fulfillment in view.

D. Jesus said there would be one generation in history in which the _____ and the _____ would mature together and culminate in a great _____.

E. A generation in Scripture ranges from:

1. Thirty to seventy years.

2. Forty to one hundred years.

3. Thirty to one hundred years.

4. Twenty to eighty years.

Small Group Discussion

A. Why did the generation during the first coming of Christ come under judgment when they did not know the time of God's visitation (Matt. 16:2–3; 21:31–32; 23:37–39; Luke 19:43–44; John 5:39–40)?

B. Why is it necessary to study the generation of the Lord's return in order to know God's heart and will (1 Chr. 12:32; Dan. 11:33; Amos 3:7–8; 1 Thess. 5:1–6; Rev. 1:1)?

C. Do you think we are presently living in the final generation before Jesus returns (Gen. 15:13–16; Num. 32:13; Ps. 90:10; Matt. 24:1–51; Acts 7:6)?

D. In the midst of the greatest revival and judgment the world has ever seen, why will multitudes still refuse to turn to God and be saved (Rom. 1:24–25; 2 Thess. 2:9–12; 1 Tim. 4:1; Heb. 3:12–13; Rev. 9:21)?

E. What are some recent events that point to an increase of "creation's groan" in the earth? How should the praying church respond to these events (Pss. 86:7; 91:15; Joel 2:12–17; Col. 1:9–11; Rev. 22:17)?

FURTHER RESOURCES

Books

Richardson, Joel. *The Islamic Antichrist: The Shocking Truth about the Real Nature of the Beast.* Los Angeles: WND Books, 2009.

Tramm, T. W. *From Abraham to Armageddon.* T. W. Tramm, 2009.

Walvoord, John and Mark Hitchcock. *Armageddon, Oil and Terror.* Carol Stream, IL: Tyndale House, 2007.

Audio

Bickle, Mike. *Knowing the Generation, but Not the Day or Hour.* October 15, 2009. http://www.MikeBickle.org.

———. *Overview: Knowing the Signs of the Times.* February 18, 2006. http://www.MikeBickle.org.

Hood, Allen. *How Can You Know You Are Living in the Last Generation? (Series).* http://www.ihop.org/store.

———. *The Uniqueness of the Last Generation (Series).* http://www.ihop.org/store.

❸ The Signs of the Times

INTRODUCTION

During these past decades, many people have written books stating that a certain event, weather pattern, or geopolitical incident was a sign of the immediate coming of the Lord and a fulfillment of scriptural prophecies. Over time, it appears that some of those predictions have not come true. Recognizing this, how do we rightly discern what is a sign of the times and what is not? What does the Bible specifically describe as end-time signs? Furthermore, do we see any of these signs in our generation? In this lesson, we will learn about the various types of end-time signs, and how the trends towards "sign events" can be watched and discerned in a valid way.

TEACHING

I. **What Are the Signs of the Times?**

There are four types of biblical "signs" that indicate when the Lord's coming is near:

A. Sign Events: These signs are *biblically predicted events* that indicate the nearness of the second coming of Jesus to the earth (Matt. 24:4–35; 2 Thess. 2:3–4). The purpose of these events is to alert the Church of the timing of His return as it relates to the need for widespread preparation and warning.

B. Sign Trends (1 John 2:18): Trends are a clear progression towards a coming sign event that can be discerned by those who take seriously the mandate of Jesus to watch and pray. For example, Paul tells us that one key sign event will be a great falling away from the faith (2 Thess. 2:3). However, this great falling away can be discerned now, in its early stages, as multitudes begin to compromise their beliefs and join a false tolerance and justice movement that is, in reality, corrupt and immoral at its core.

C. Cosmic Signs: These signs are *dramatic* and *highly unusual phenomena* that are *predicted in Scripture* (Matt. 24:29; Acts 2:19–20). The purpose of these cosmic signs (i.e. unusual weather patterns or "signs in the heavens") is to communicate to unbelievers in a powerful, dramatic way that the wrath and judgment of God is coming.

D. Personal Signs: These are subjective, prophetic experiences that alert, encourage, and exhort believers related to the end times. These are not to be communicated in a public manner, except for rare circumstances, but are for the personal edification and preparation of the believer (Amos 3:7–8; Acts 2:17).

E. With regard to studying the signs of the times, it is critical to acknowledge that in the past few decades there has been a poorly-timed emphasis on biblical signs related to current events. Past studies pertaining to the signs of the times often involved inadequate, imprecise conclusions from current events with few solid, credible scriptural connections.[12] At the same time, it is important to acknowledge the courage with which these bold voices served their generation by igniting exploration of a topic so clearly ignored by the Body of Christ.

F. As we learn from one another's weaknesses and errors, we are able to pursue an understanding of the signs that Jesus commanded us to study and watch for in a manner that is scripturally accurate, rather than abandoning the topic altogether.

II. Trends towards Positive "Sign Events" within the Church

A. Sign Event: The gospel of the kingdom will be preached in every nation.

And this gospel of the kingdom will be preached in <u>all the world</u> as a witness to all the nations, and then the end will come. (Matt. 24:14)

1. The book of Revelation tells us that a remnant of believers will come forth from every tribe, tongue, people, and nation before the judgment events of the end times.

---

12 In the early 1970s, the pretribulation rapture viewpoint exploded across the Body of Christ, leading to the publication of many books that captured the imagination of the Church by connecting current events to biblical passages. One example of this practice was to equate the "European Community," which grew from six nations to nine during that decade, to the "ten-nation coalition" spoken of in Revelation 17:7. When it became twelve nations in 1986, much of the energy was drained from the discussion of Europe's role in the end times. In its current form, it is called the "European Union" and includes twenty-seven states.

And they sang a new song, saying: "You are worthy to take the scroll, and to open its seals; for You were slain, and have redeemed us to God by Your blood out of every tribe and tongue and people and nation." (Rev. 5:9)

2. For the first time in history, it is possible that every tribe, tongue, people, and nation will have a witness of the gospel within a generation. By most conservative estimates, this could be the generation that will see the earth evangelized.

    a. Stephen Douglass, the President of Campus Crusade for Christ (the largest mission organization in the world), announced at the Call2All International Congress in Dayton, Ohio, in January 2009, that he believes the Great Commission will be fulfilled within his lifetime—possibly within the next ten years.[13]

    b. As of the end of 2007, it is estimated that 4.8 billion people have been evangelized, the Bible has been translated into 6,600 languages and is available to 95.6% of the world's population,[14] and churches exist in all 238 nations and territories of the earth.[15]

    c. We are in the time of the greatest harvest of souls in church history. In 1800, at the beginning of the Protestant Missions Movement, nearly 75% of the global population had never heard the gospel. As of 2007, after the global population had multiplied seven times, only 25% of the global population remained unevangelized.[16]

---

13 "Fulfilling the Great Commission," Christian Today, last modified January 27, 2009, http://www.christiantoday.com/article/fulfilling.the.great.commission/22389.htm.

14 David B. Barrett, Todd M. Johnson, and Peter F. Crossing, "Missiometrics 2008: Reality Checks for Christian World Communions," *International Bulletin of Missionary Research* 32:1 (January 2008): 27–30.

15 David B. Barrett and Todd M. Johnson, "Global Diagram 34. Today's global mission: the status of world evangelization in AD 2000.," in *World Christian Trends*, ed. Christopher R. Guidry and Peter F. Crossing (Pasadena: William Carey Library, 2001), http://www.gem-werc.org/gd/gd34.pdf (accessed December 7, 2010).

16 David B. Barrett, Todd M. Johnson, and Peter F. Crossing, "Missiometrics 2007: Creating Your Own Analysis of Global Data," *International Bulletin of Missionary Research* 31:1 (January 2007): 25–32.

d. Over the past thirty years, the number of people watching and listening to Christian television and radio has exploded from 22% of the world to 39%. The gospel is going forth and hearts are responding in historic numbers.[17]

e. The Wycliffe Bible Society launched their "Vision 2025" in 1999 with a goal of translating the Bible into every known language by 2025. In 1999, they were at a rate of completing a translation every eighteen days. By 2008, the rate had increased to a translation every five days.[18]

f. Since its release in 1979, the "Jesus Film" has been seen in every country and territory in the world—more regions than FedEx can deliver to (220), or Coca-Cola can reach (200).[19] Several billion people have viewed the film,[20] with a decision for Christ being made every eight seconds somewhere around the world, totaling more than 200 million decisions for Christ.[21]

B. Sign Event: The Jewish leadership of Jerusalem and all of Israel will experience revival, repentance, and salvation.

O Jerusalem, Jerusalem, . . . [39]I say to you, you shall see Me no more till you say, "Blessed is He who comes in the name of the LORD!" (Matt. 23:37–39)

I say then, have they stumbled that they should fall? Certainly not! But through their fall, to provoke them to jealousy, salvation has come to the Gentiles. [12]Now if their fall is riches for the world, and their failure riches for the Gentiles, how much more their fullness! (Rom. 11:11–12)

---

17 David B. Barrett, Todd M. Johnson, and Peter F. Crossing, "Missiometrics 2008: Reality Checks for Christian World Communions," *International Bulletin of Missionary Research* 32:1 (January 2008): 27–30.

18 "When We'll Finish: Vision 2025," Wycliffe Bible Translators, accessed December 6, 2010, http://www.wycliffe.org/Explore/WhenWillWeFinishtheTask. aspx.

19 "The JESUS Film Project," Campus Crusade For Christ International, accessed November 29, 2010, http://www.ccci.org/ministries-and-locations/ministries/the-jesus-film-project/index.htm.

20 "The Official Ministry Statistics of The JESUS Film Project," The JESUS Film Project, accessed November 29, 2010, http://www.jesusfilm.org/film-and-media/statistics/quarterly-statistics.

21 The JESUS Film Project, accessed November 29, 2010, http://www.jesusfilm.org/.

For I do not desire, brethren, that you should be ignorant of this mystery, lest you should be wise in your own opinion, that blindness in part has happened to Israel until the fullness of the Gentiles has come in. ²⁶And so all Israel will be saved. (Rom. 11:25–26)

1. One necessary precondition for this sign event (and for several others) is the reconstitution of the nation of Israel with Jewish leadership in their ancient homeland. It is remarkable that after 1,900 years without a homeland, the Jewish people are back in the land of Israel as a sovereign state (1948) with Jerusalem as their capital city (1967). Even more remarkable is that this has transpired in the same generation that world evangelization will be completed (i.e. the fullness of the Gentiles coming in).

2. Jewish Messianic congregations in Israel are experiencing more growth through conversions than at any time in church history since the first century.

   a. In a survey of Messianic believers in Israel conducted in 1999, the number of congregations had increased from two in 1948 to eighty-one. The number of Jewish believers had, in that time, increased from less than 200 believers to 2,178 believers.[22]

   b. It is estimated that there are currently up to 120 Messianic congregations in the land of Israel comprising between 10,000 and 15,000 individuals.[23] In other words, the number of congregations has increased by 50%. Despite the fact that Israel is one of the most difficult nations in which to preach the gospel (Rom. 11:7–10), the number of believers in Israel has increased by nearly 700% in nine years.

C. Sign Event: There will be a global outpouring of the Holy Spirit on young and old believers everywhere just before the return

---

22 Kai Kjaer-Hansen & Bodil F. Skjøtt, *Facts & Myths about Messianic Congregations in Israel* (Jerusalem: Caspari Center for Biblical and Jewish Studies, 1999), 17, quoted in Jeffrey S. Wasserman, *Messianic Jewish Congregations: Who Sold this Business to the Gentiles?* (Lanham, MD: University Press of America, 2000), ix.

23 "Israel's Messianic Jews: Some Call it a Miracle," CBN News, last modified December 26, 2008, http://www.cbn.com/cbnnews/insideisrael/2008/December/Israels-Messianic-Jews-Some-Call-it-a-Miracle-/.

of Jesus. This will lead to an unprecedented level of prophecy, dreams, and visions.

And it shall come to pass in the last days, says God, <u>that I will pour out of My Spirit on all flesh; your sons and your daughters shall prophesy</u>, your young men shall see visions, your old men shall dream dreams. [18]And on My menservants and on My maidservants I will pour out My Spirit in those days; and they shall prophesy. . . . [20]<u>before the coming of the great and awesome day of the LORD</u>. (Acts 2:17–20)

1. The number of Pentecostal and charismatic believers has jumped from one million in 1900 to 602 million today. This indicates an increased pursuit of the gifts and power of the Holy Spirit in every denomination of Christianity.[24]

2. The widespread, supernatural activity in this hour is unique, with one of the signs being transformed cities and revival centers across the world. This spike in the manifestations of the Spirit's power throughout the Church is unique in its scope and impact.[25]

D. Sign Event: There will be a night-and-day prayer and worship movement across the earth that brings about "speedy justice" at the second coming.

And shall God not avenge His own elect who <u>cry out day and night to Him</u>, though He bears long with them? [8]I tell you that <u>He will avenge them speedily</u>. Nevertheless, <u>when the Son of Man comes</u>, will He really find faith on the earth? (Luke 18:7–8)

And the <u>Spirit and the bride</u> say, "<u>Come!</u>" (Rev. 22:17)

1. Scripture prophesies the emergence of a global prayer and worship movement that will be marked by enjoyable prayer (Isa. 56:7). Joel 2:15 and Zephaniah 2:3 call believers

---

24 David B. Barrett, Todd M. Johnson, and Peter F. Crossing, "Missiometrics 2008: Reality Checks for Christian World Communions," *International Bulletin of Missionary Research* 32:1 (January 2008): 27–30.

25 George Otis Jr. (www.glowtorch.org) has produced several documentaries that show how people groups, cities, and nations have been transformed through repentance and the healing presence of God: *Transformations: A Documentary* (Lynnwood, WA: The Sentinel Group, 1999), *Transformations II: The Glory Spreads* (2001), *An Unconventional War* (2007), *A Force for Change* (2009), and *Appalachian Dawn* (2010).

to gather and participate in solemn assemblies of fasting, prayer, and repentance related to the coming judgments.

2. Throughout Scripture, a widespread explosion of music and worship is pictured as related to the Church's agreement with and joy in the end-time plans of God. The current explosion of prayer with music is a sign of what was predicted thousands of years ago regarding the people of God at the time of the return of Jesus (Ps. 149:1–9; Isa. 42:10; Jer. 31:7; Rev. 5:8–12).

3. The stirring of the Lord to gather thousands for stadium prayer meetings, and the emergence of prayer ministries throughout the earth, is a sign of the times. Two examples of this are the emergence and growth of the Global Day of Prayer over the last eight years,[26] and the recognition of the need for corporate prayer to complete the evangelization of the nations.[27]

4. For the first time in thousands of years, houses of prayer are established in the city of Jerusalem, devoted to night-and-day intercession for the revival of that city, similar to what Isaiah prophesied (62:6).

III. Trends towards Negative "Sign Events" within the Church

A. Sign Event: There will be incredible persecution against believers in a manner that will be unprecedented in all of church history (Dan. 7:21, 25; 8:24; 11:33–35; 12:7, 10; Matt. 10:21–22, 28; Luke 12:4–7; 21:16–19; Rev. 6:9–11; 7:9, 14; 11:7; 13:7, 15; 16:5–6; 18:24; 19:2).

---

26 In March 2001, more than 45,000 Christians united for a "Day of Repentance and Prayer" at Newlands Rugby Stadium in Cape Town. By May 2008, participation in the event had grown to millions of individuals covering 214 nations of the earth. "History," Global Day of Prayer, accessed December 2, 2010, http://www.globaldayofprayer.com/history.html.

27 One of the six main themes of the Call2All congresses on world evangelization includes working with the Global Prayer Movement. At the October 2008 Call2All congress in Kenya, missions organizations, pastors, and leaders committed to establish 75,000 houses of prayer globally over the next ten years. "The Global Prayer And Missions Movements Join Hands," Call2All, last modified February 28, 2008, http://www.call2all.org/Articles/1000028668/Call2All/About_Us/E_zine_Archive/2008/The_Prayer_And.aspx.

Then they will deliver you up to tribulation and kill you, and <u>you will be hated by all nations for My name's sake</u>. (Matt. 24:9)

I saw the woman [Harlot Babylon], <u>drunk with the blood of the saints</u> and with the blood of the martyrs of Jesus. (Rev. 17:6)

1. Persecution has increased exponentially in the twentieth and twenty-first centuries compared to other eras of church history, as documented by the Voice of the Martyrs organization.[28]

2. According to the World Christian Encyclopedia (2001), the number of martyrs recorded over 1,900 years of church history equaled 24.6 million. In the twentieth century, however, there were 45.4 million martyrs across the earth.[29]

B. Sign Event: There will be a great falling away from the faith. Widespread heresy will sweep across the Church as many false teachers and false prophets emerge at the end of the age, leading to an unprecedented apostasy, or mass exodus, from the Church and from faith in Christ (1 Tim. 4:1–4; 2 Tim. 3:5).

And because lawlessness will abound, <u>the love of many will grow cold.</u> ¹³But he who endures to the end shall be saved. (Matt. 24:12–13)

Let no one deceive you by any means; for <u>that Day will not come unless the falling away comes first</u>. (2 Thess. 2:3)

1. There is a trend across the Body of Christ, of leniency toward immoral behavior, church governance, and practices that are in direct contradiction to Scripture. Many churches are denying Scripture as the authoritative, infallible, and inerrant source of truth.

---

28 *Voice of the Martyrs* is a non-profit, interdenominational Christian organization dedicated to assisting the persecuted church worldwide. Their website (http://www.persecution.com) has current news reports and practical ways that you can help believers worldwide who are suffering for the name of Christ.

29 David B. Barrett and Todd M. Johnson, "Global Diagram 16. Evangelization through martyrdom: 70 million Christians killed for their faith in 220 countries across 20 centuries," in *World Christian Trends*, ed. Christopher R. Guidry and Peter F. Crossing (Pasadena: William Carey Library, 2001), http://www.gordon-conwell.edu/resources/documents/gd16.pdf (accessed November 16, 2011).

2. Other recent examples of the growing decline of biblical Christianity include the ordination of homosexuals and the support for homosexual marriage, the denial of the deity of Christ, and the denial of Christ as the only way of salvation.

IV. Trends toward Sign Events in Israel

One of the most significant prophetic signs is the re-emergence of Israel as a political state in 1948, an historic development that became even more established with the Six-Day War and the re-unification of Jerusalem in June 1967. This set the stage for the fulfillment of hundreds of prophetic scriptures related to the nation of Israel that had now become relevant for the first time in nearly 1,900 years. In particular, the following are significant sign events related to the nation of Israel:

A. Jerusalem will be surrounded by hostile nations and will be the apex of world controversy. The Bible describes Jerusalem in the latter days as inhabited by citizens of the state of Israel and surrounded by every nation as they gather to make war against her (Joel 3:2, 12; Zeph. 3:8; Zech. 12:1–3; 14:1–3; Luke 21:5–36).

B. Jerusalem will become the central focus of world attention.

And it shall happen in that day that I will make Jerusalem ta very heavy stone for __all peoples__; all who would heave it away will surely be cut in pieces, though __all nations__ of the earth are gathered against it [Jerusalem]. (Zech. 12:3)

I will gather __all the nations__ to battle against Jerusalem. (Zech. 14:2)

C. A Middle East peace treaty with Israel will be brokered by the Antichrist (Dan. 9:27; 1 Thess. 5:2–3).

D. A rebuilt temple in Jerusalem will be desecrated by the Antichrist (Dan. 9:27; 11:36–45; Matt. 24:15; Mark 13:14; 2 Thess. 2:4; Rev. 11:1–2).

V. Other Significant Sign Trends

A. There will be unmatched interest about the end of the age and in end-time prophecy (Jer. 30:24; Dan. 11:33; 12:10). An angel told

Daniel that information about the end of the age was sealed in his day, only to be unveiled at the time of the end (Dan. 12:4, 9–10).

The anger of the LORD will not turn back until He has executed and performed the thoughts of His heart. <u>In the latter days you will understand it perfectly</u>. (Jer. 23:20)

B. A great increase in knowledge through technological advances will occur. With the present popularity and availability of the Internet and satellite communications, there has never been an era like the one we live in, as related to the ease of obtaining information and knowledge.

Seal the book until the time of the end; many shall run to and fro, and <u>knowledge shall increase</u>. (Dan. 12:4)

C. Globalization and global political alliances will escalate. The Bible has much to say about globalization and the manner in which finances, commerce, communication, religion, and geopolitics will converge from nation-based contexts to a more globally unified expression. These will culminate in a demonically-empowered, global worship movement (Rev. 13:1–18; 17:1–18:24). According to the Bible, nations and religions will join together to pool resources and power for economic and spiritual reasons.

D. The movement of nations against Israel, and the unification of nations globally, through political, economic, and military alliances, are vividly described in prophecies about the end times. The most challenging issues facing nations are international in nature, including global warming, the global war on terror, and the global financial crisis. The tension in the financial crisis is that we have global financial markets without global rule of law. The growing crisis in these three issues is changing the political atmosphere, so that "global governance" is a more attractive solution to global problems.

E. Some of the following developments could point toward this movement:

1. The unification of nations in the same territory as the ancient Roman Empire (Dan. 2:41–42; 7:7, 20, 24; 9:27; Rev. 12:3; 13:1; 17:3, 7, 12, 16).

2. A movement toward a one-world economy (Rev. 13:16–18; 18:1–24).

3. The rebuilding of the city of Babylon (Jer. 50:1–51:64; Rev. 17:1–18:24).[30]

4. Plans in Israel to rebuild the Jerusalem temple (2 Thess. 2:3–4).[31]

5. Microchip technology that facilitates the "mark of the beast" economic system (Rev. 13:16–17).[32]

VI. Twelve Future Sign Trends (Matt. 24:4–8; Luke 21:7–18)

Jesus . . . said to them: "Take heed that no one deceives you. ⁵For many will come in My name, saying, 'I am the Christ,' and will deceive many. ⁶And you will hear of wars and rumors of wars. See that you are not troubled; . . . the end is not yet. ⁷For nation will rise against nation, and kingdom against kingdom. And there will be famines, pestilences, and earthquakes in various places. ⁸All these are the beginning of sorrows." (Matt. 24:4–8)

A. Jesus spoke of twelve sign trends, referred to as "the beginning of sorrows" or "birth-pangs," that would occur in the period leading up to the final time of tribulation, culminating in the Lord's return.

---

30 It is widely recognized that Saddam Hussein was working on rebuilding the ancient city of Babylon before his death. "Saddam's Babylonian Palace," About.com, accessed December 3, 2010, http://architecture.about.com/cs/countriescultures/a/saddamspalace.htm. Since his passing, the government of Iraq is actively trying to preserve remains from the city as a tourist attraction. "Iraq tourism hangs in balance at Babylon," CNN, last modified January 14, 2011, http://edition.cnn.com/2011/WORLD/meast/01/13/babylon.iraq.archaeology/.

31 "The Temple Institute . . . , founded in 1987, is a non-profit educational and religious organization located in the Jewish quarter of Jerusalem's Old City. . . . The major focus of the Institute is its efforts towards the beginning of the actual rebuilding of the Holy Temple. Towards this end, the Institute has begun to restore and construct the sacred vessels for the service of the Holy Temple." "About the Temple Institute," The Temple Institute, accessed December 3, 2010, http://www.templeinstitute.org/about.htm.

32 "India Launches Project to ID 1.2 Billion People," Wall Street Journal, last modified September 29, 2010, http://online.wsj.com/article/SB10001424052748704652104575493490951809322.html#ixzz1FNXdz9Kk. "The Next Generation May Be 'Chipped,'" PCWorld, last modified June 12, 2010, http://www.pcworld.com/article/198664/the_next_generation_may_be_chipped.html.

B. Seven are mentioned in Matthew 24 (false christs, war, ethnic conflict, economic warfare, famines, pestilences, and earthquakes), and a further five are revealed in Luke 21 (commotions, fearful sights, great signs from heaven, distress in the nations, and roaring waves). Jesus exhorted the generation of believers who would witness these signs to, "see that you are not troubled; for all these things must come to pass, but the end is not yet" (Matt. 24:6).

1. *Many will come in My name, saying, "I am the Christ," and will deceive many. (Matt. 24:5)*

    The context has been established in Israel for many to emerge as false political "messiahs" who, in the minds of some, will help deliver Israel from her enemies and establish Torah as national law again.

2. *You will hear of wars and rumors of wars (Matt. 24:6–7)*

    In the twentieth century alone, over one hundred million people were killed in war.[33]

3. *There will be famines (Matt. 24:7)*

    According to the Food and Agriculture Organization of the United Nations, 864 million people worldwide were undernourished in 2002–2004.[34] In 2007, one in every three people in Sub-Saharan Africa was undernourished. Famine also afflicted South Asia with a reported 299 million being underfed; this was followed by East Asia with 225 million.[35]

---

33 Precise numbers are not possible to ascertain, though the following resources are helpful: Milton Leitenberg, "Deaths in Wars and Conflicts in the 20th Century, 3rd ed. " (Peace Studies Program, Cornell, 2006), 14, http://www.cissm.umd.edu/papers/files/deathswarsconflictsjune52006.pdf. See also "Deaths by Mass Unpleasantness: Estimated Totals for the Entire 20th Century," Twentieth Century Atlas—Worldwide Statistics of Casualties, Massacres, Disasters and Atrocities, last modified March 25, 2003, http://users.erols.com/mwhite28/warstat8.htm.

34 World Bank, *Atlas of Global Development 2nd Edition* (Glasglow: Gollins Geo., 2009), http://issuu.com/world.bank.publications/docs/atlas2/13/ (accessed November 30, 2010).

35 "World Development Report 2008: Agriculture for Development, 94," (Wash, DC: The World Bank, 2007), http://siteresources.worldbank.org/INTWDR2008/Resources/WDR_00_book.pdf (accessed November 30, 2010).

4. *Pestilences (Matt. 24:7)*

Over two hundred different kinds of cancer[36] kill an estimated 7.6 million people per year.[37] The AIDS virus alone
has killed an estimated 25 million worldwide.[38] Over the
last several years, the world has witnessed many new
infectious viruses, or "super bugs" (e.g. the bird flu or
H5N1, SARS, the Ebola virus, and MRSA). These diseases
are unique in how rapidly they spread and how difficult
they are to treat. Many experts agree that, due to global-
ized travel, the trading of food and goods, and "the ability
of the influenza virus to reassort genes," a great poten-
tial exists for a serious pandemic that will kill millions of
people.[39] One expert writes, "The world has rapidly become much more vulnerable to the eruption and, most
critically, to the widespread and even global spread of
both new and old infectious diseases."[40]

5. *Earthquakes in various places (Matt. 24:7)*

Earthquakes will continually increase in severity as we
get nearer to the end. These earthquakes, like the increase in famine and pestilence, will shift the global
mood drastically, and heighten desperation for societal
change in vast numbers of people.

---

36 "A to Z List of Cancers," National Cancer Institute, accessed December 1, 2010,
http://www.cancer.gov/cancertopics/types/alphalist.

37 "Global Cancer Facts & Figures 2007," American Cancer Society, accessed December 3, 2010, http://www.cancer.org/acs/groups/content/@nho/documents/
document/globalfactsandfigures2007rev2p.pdf.

38 "Global Facts and Figures 09," Joint United Nations Programme on HIV/
AIDs, accessed December 1, 2010, http://data.unaids.org/pub/Fact-
Sheet/2009/20091124_FS_global_en.pdf.

39 John M. Barry, *The Great Influenza: The Epic Story of the Deadliest Plague in History* (New York: Penguin Group, 2004), 449.

40 Laurie Garrett, *The Coming Plague: Newly Emerging Diseases in a World Out of
Balance* (New York: Farrar, Straus and Giroux, 1994), xi. Also see Madeline Drex-
ler, *Secret Agents: the Menace of Emerging Infections* (Washington: Joseph Henry
Press, 2002); "The Next Pandemic," The Daily Beast, last modified May 3, 2009,
http://www.thedailybeast.com/newsweek/2009/05/03/the-next-pandemic.html;
and *John M. Barry, The Great Influenza: The Story of the Deadliest Pandemic in
History* (New York: Penguin Books, 2005).

VII. How Then Shall We Live?

Understanding the signs of the times should fill us with an urgency to cultivate a lifestyle of prayer. If we do, we will be able to prepare others for these end-time events which will otherwise leave multitudes offended by God. Along these lines, each of Jesus' teachings on the signs of the times concludes with an exhortation to watch and pray, because the Day of the Lord will come as a snare on the whole earth. We must be diligent to study the drama of the end times, and allow our hearts to be fascinated by the perfect leadership of Jesus.

But <u>take heed to yourselves</u>, lest your hearts be weighed down with carousing, drunkenness, and cares of this life, and that Day come on you unexpectedly. [35]For <u>it will come as a snare on all those who dwell on the face of the whole earth</u>. (Luke 21:34–35)

You therefore, beloved, <u>since you know this beforehand, beware lest you also fall from your own steadfastness</u>, being led away with the error of the wicked; [18]but grow in the grace and knowledge of our Lord and Savior Jesus Christ. To Him be the glory both now and forever. Amen. (2 Pet. 3:17–18)

SUMMARY

Throughout the day, you check your watch or cell phone to see what time it is. Based on what time it is, you know what to do next. When it is eight in the morning, you go to work; when it is noon, you go to lunch; when it is five in the afternoon, you drive back home. On the other hand, if you never knew what time it was, you would never be able to make the right decisions or take the right actions. If this is true for your life individually, is it not also true for the Church globally? It is imperative that we rightly discern the scriptural signs of the times and know our place at this stage of history.

QUESTIONS

Reviewing (see answers on page 98)

A. Which of the following sign trends in the Church will precede the return of Jesus?

1. The unprecedented evangelization of the earth.

2. The sealing of the Lord's servants, protecting them from persecution.

3. The completing of the Great Commission through the full conversion of all nations.

4. The widespread compromise of the faith by many believers.

B. The book of Revelation tells us that a remnant of believers will come forth from every _____, _____, _____, and _____ before the judgment events of the end times.

C. True or False—There will be persecution against believers in a manner that will be unique in all of church history.

D. There will be widespread _____ in the Church as many false teachers and false prophets emerge at the end of the age, leading to unprecedented _____.

E. For the first time in thousands of years, houses of prayer are established in the city of Jerusalem, similar to the prophecy by which Old Testament prophet:

1. Elijah

2. Zechariah

3. Joel

4. Isaiah

Small Group Discussion

A. Given the reality of Matthew 24:14 and Revelation 5:9, how can you practically help to establish a gospel witness in places there is presently no witness (Matt. 10:37–38; 28:18–20; Rom. 15:20; Col. 4:2–3; 2 Thess. 3:1–2)? In what ways can you spend your time, money, and energy to help reach the lost (Matt. 5:2–7:27; Rom. 12:4–8; 1 Cor. 12:1–11; Col. 3:17, 23)?

B. Is the trend towards globalization and an escalation of global, political alliances a positive or negative trend (Dan. 2:41–42; 7:7, 20, 24; 9:27; 12:4; Rev. 13:1–18; 17:1–18:24)?

C. Why was the re-establishing of the nation of Israel such a significant event pointing to the signs of the times (Jer. 30:3; Ezek. 34:11–13; 36:23–28; Zech. 14:1–4; Matt. 23:37–39; Luke 21:20)?

D. How can you help combat the present trend in the Church towards biblical leniency and a distortion of the truth (2 Thess. 2:15; 1 Tim. 4:1–4; 2 Tim. 2:15; 3:5–7; Heb. 2:1–3; Rev. 12:11)?

E. Why should personal signs (subjective, prophetic experiences) related to the end times usually not be broadcast or communicated in a public manner (2 Cor. 12:1–4; Gal. 1:11–12)?

FURTHER RESOURCES

Audio

Bickle, Mike. *Knowing the Signs of the Times Part 1.* December 12, 2008. http://www.MikeBickle.org.

———. *Knowing the Signs of the Times Part 2.* December 13, 2008. http://www.MikeBickle.org.

———. *Negative Trends, People and Events in the End Times.* December 2, 2005. http://www.MikeBickle.org.

———. *Political Signs of the Times Pertaining to the Nation of Israel.* February 25, 2006. http://www.MikeBickle.org.

———. *Positive Trends, People and Events in the End Times.* December 2, 2005. http://www.MikeBickle.org.

———. *Sign Events and Trends in Gentile Nations.* November 7, 2009. http://www.MikeBickle.org.

———. *Understanding What Is Happening in the Middle East.* July 23, 2006. http://www.MikeBickle.org.

④ Overview of the End Times

INTRODUCTION

Have you ever put together a large jigsaw puzzle? With so many pieces spread out over the table, how do you begin? The best way is to first connect the pieces comprising the frame. Once the frame is set up, it is significantly easier to know where the rest of the pieces go. In the same way, once you know the overall framework and context of the end times, the details begin to make sense. Not only will the scriptural teachings on the end times become more understandable, but the panoramic story of the entire Bible will become clearer as well. In this lesson, we will explore an overview of the end times, including the key scriptural passages, main events, and basic chronology.

TEACHING

I. **Jesus Is Coming to Take Over the Kingdoms of the Earth**

A. God's ultimate purpose for the earth is to restore everything that was lost in the garden of Eden. He will reunite heaven and earth as Jesus establishes His kingdom over all the earth (Dan. 2:44; Eph. 1:9; Rev. 11:15). Jesus will prepare the earth for the rule of His Father at the end of the millennial kingdom (1 Cor. 15:20–28; Rev. 21:3).

B. At His first coming, Jesus did not rule as an earthly king, but came as a servant to conquer sin and death (Heb. 12:2). He came to sacrifice His life for the sins of the world (Heb. 10:5–12). Having been resurrected from the dead, He is currently seated at the right hand of God's throne, and ever lives to make intercession for His people (Heb. 7:25).

C. When Jesus returns, He will enforce the authority that He won on the cross and make all of His enemies a footstool under His feet (Heb. 10:13). He will rule all the nations with a rod of iron and take over all the kingdoms of the earth (Pss. 2:9; 110:2; Rev. 2:26; 11:15).

D. Jesus declared that all authority in heaven and earth had been given to Him (Matt. 28:18). The transition of power at the end of the age is described as a violent revolution, as Jesus confronts the Antichrist's empire and the rebellious kings of the earth who actively resist His leadership (Ps. 2:1–12; Rev. 2:26–27; 19:15)

Why do the nations rage, and the people plot a vain thing? ²The kings of the earth set themselves, and the rulers take counsel together, against the LORD and against His Anointed, saying, ³"Let us break their bonds in pieces and cast away their cords from us." ⁴He who sits in the heavens shall laugh; the LORD shall hold them in derision. ⁵Then He shall speak to them in His wrath, and distress them in His deep displeasure: ⁶"Yet I have set My King on My holy hill of Zion. ⁷I will declare the decree: the LORD has said to Me, 'You are My Son, today I have begotten You. ⁸Ask of Me, and I will give You [Jesus] the nations for Your inheritance, and the ends of the earth for Your possession. ⁹You shall break them with a rod of iron; you shall dash them to pieces like a potter's vessel.'" (Ps. 2:1–9)

II. **What Is the Day of the Lord?**

Blow the trumpet in Zion, and sound an alarm in My holy mountain! Let all the inhabitants of the land tremble; for the day of the LORD is coming. (Joel 2:1)

For the day of the LORD is great and very terrible; who can endure it? (Joel 2:11; cf. Mal. 3:2; 4:5)

A. The *Day of the Lord* is a unique time period when God's blessings and judgments will be openly manifest in an exceptional way. There are two expressions of the Day of the Lord: a historical lesser day, and a global ultimate Day.

B. Throughout Scripture, God primarily uses two Old Testament events to illustrate the historical lesser day: the story of Moses in Exodus, and the Babylonian military invasion in 586 BC. These two events point to a future Day of the Lord at the end of the age, when similar judgments will be released with greater intensity on a global level.

C. The global ultimate Day of the Lord can be understood in both a "broad" and a "narrow" sense. In the broad sense, the Day of the Lord encompasses all the end-time events commencing with the Great Tribulation, and culminating with the final judgment and the descent of the New Jerusalem to the earth. In the narrow sense, it is a literal, twenty-four-hour period of time, describing when Jesus returns as King to Jerusalem (Zech. 14:3–4).

But the heavens and the earth which are now preserved by the same word, are reserved for fire until the <u>day of judgment</u> and perdition of ungodly men. ⁸But, beloved, <u>do not forget this one thing, that with the Lord one day is as a thousand years</u>, and <u>a thousand years as one day.</u> (2 Pet. 3:7–8)

D. The Day of the Lord will be the most dramatic period of human history. It will not mark the end of the world, as some have concluded. Rather, it will mark the beginning of a new age with the reign of God on the earth. The dramatic nature of the end-time events led Jesus to liken the end-time drama to the labor pains experienced in childbirth (Matt. 24:8; Mark 13:8, NASB). Women have described the process of giving birth as the most painful and intense thing they have ever experienced. This same level of intensity and pain will mark the Day of Lord, but we must remember that, for the Church, the pain will produce indescribable glory.

E. One of the best ways to understand the Day of the Lord is to take a look at the primary framework, events, and people of this great, end-time drama.

III. The Basic Framework

A. The books of Daniel and Revelation provide more information on the events surrounding the return of Jesus than any other books in Scripture. Understanding the sequence of events revealed in Daniel 9 is critical to understanding the timing of events that are described in more detail elsewhere in Scripture, particularly in the book of Revelation.

B. In response to Daniel's prayer and fasting, the angel Gabriel gave Daniel an overview of Israel's future that provides a basic framework and timeline for all the events of the end times. The end goal of this timeline is the salvation of Israel and the establishing of the Messiah's kingdom over all the earth.

And after the sixty-two weeks Messiah shall be cut off, but not for Himself; and the people of the prince who is to come shall destroy the city and the sanctuary. The end of it shall be with a flood, and till the end of the war desolations are determined. ²⁷Then he shall confirm a covenant with many for one week; but in the middle of the week he shall bring an end to sacrifice and offering. And on the wing of abominations shall be one who makes desolate, even until the consummation, which is determined, is poured out on the desolate. (Dan. 9:26–27)

C. In summary, Daniel was told the following:

1. The focus of God's plan is the nation of Israel (9:24).

2. It will take seventy "weeks" or "sevens" to complete this plan. A "week" or "seven" can be a period of seven days, months, or years. In this context, it is referring to a period of seven years (9:24).

3. The following objectives will be achieved over the course of this 490-year period: God's judgment of Israel will be satisfied, provision will be made for her sin, Israel will be forgiven, all prophecy will be fulfilled (Acts 3:21), and everlasting righteousness will be established from Israel (9:24).

4. The seventy "sevens" will begin with a command to rebuild Jerusalem, which will occur in difficult times (9:25).

5. From the command to rebuild Jerusalem until the ministry of the Messiah, there will be a total of sixty-nine "sevens" or 483 years (9:25).

6. At some point *after* the first sixty-nine "sevens," the following will happen: the Messiah will be "cut off," or killed, the city of Jerusalem and the temple will be destroyed by "the people of the prince who is to come," and Jerusalem will be left desolate "till the end of the war" (9:26).

7. The "prince who is to come" will make a covenant with Israel for one "week" or seven years (9:27).

8. He will bring an end to sacrifices and offerings in the middle of that "week" (seven years), and establish something abominable in its place. This presupposes that a temple in Jerusalem will be rebuilt, for sacrifices must be offered in a temple.[41]

9. At the end of the seven years, the abomination will be judged, and the righteous reign of the Messiah will begin (9:24, 27).

D. Daniel was given an overview of Israel's future from his own day until the return of Jesus. Much of this prophecy has already been fulfilled with stunning accuracy, as described below.

1. Many scholars agree that the time from the decree to rebuild Jerusalem until the start of Jesus' ministry (approximately AD 27) was 483 years (9:25).[42]

2. *After* the first 483 years, or sixty-nine "sevens" (seven "sevens," plus sixty-two "sevens"), the following events occurred: in approximately AD 29, Jesus died ("not for Himself," but for the sin of the whole world), Jerusalem was made desolate (including the destruction of the temple) by Rome in AD 70, its people were dispersed, and the city has been subjected to much conflict and war since that time (9:26).

3. With the exception of Jesus' death, all these events took place more than seven years after the beginning of His ministry. Thus, it appears that there is a substantial "gap" between the first sixty-nine "sevens," and the final "seven."

4. Many commentators, who adopt a "futurist" view of prophetic scripture, agree that Daniel's final "seven" is a seven-year period that will directly precede the return of Jesus and the salvation of Israel.[43] This seven-year period is the final "seven," or "week," referenced at the end of Daniel 9.

---

41 Gleason L. Archer Jr., "Daniel," in *The Expositor's Bible Commentary*, ed. Frank E. Gaebelein, vol. 7 (Grand Rapids, MI: Zondervan, 1985), 117; John F. Walvoord, *Daniel: The Key to Prophetic Revelation* (Chicago: Moody Press, 1971), 237.

42 Stephen R. Miller, *Daniel*, New American Commentary, vol. 18 (Nashville: Broadman & Holman, 1994), 265–66; Walvoord, 223–28; Archer Jr., 113–16.

43 Miller, 269; Walvoord, 232, 236–37; Archer, 117.

IV. Understanding Daniel's "Seventieth Week"

Then he [the prince who is to come] shall confirm a covenant with many for one week; but in the middle of the week he shall bring an end to sacrifice and offering. And on the wing of abominations shall be one who makes desolate, even until the consummation, which is determined, is poured out on the desolate. (Dan. 9:27)

A. The beginning of the seventieth, or final "week," is marked by a covenant that is brokered by the "prince who is to come." This covenant signals the end of Israel's desolations, and is thus presumed to be some kind of peace treaty, allowing a Jewish temple to be rebuilt and sacrifices to take place in Jerusalem. The peace treaty initiates the beginning of a seven-year period that will culminate with the return of Jesus and the salvation of Israel.

B. The first half of this final, seven-year "week" is characterized by false peace and safety. However, the covenant is broken at the three-and-a-half-year mark (in the middle of the "week"), when the "prince who is to come" brings an end to temple sacrifices, and sets up an abomination in the holy place of the temple. Jesus refers to this event as marking the beginning of the Great Tribulation.

Therefore when you see the "abomination of desolation," spoken of by Daniel the prophet, standing in the holy place (whoever reads, let him understand), ¹⁶then let those who are in Judea flee to the mountains. . . . ²¹For then there will be great tribulation, such as has not been since the beginning of the world until this time, no, nor ever shall be. (Matt. 24:15–16, 21)

C. Paul identifies the "prince who is to come" as "the man of sin," elsewhere called "the Antichrist."[44] He tells us that this man, described as "another horn, a little one" in Daniel 7:8, will sit in the Jerusalem temple, as God, and demand worship. This is the very essence of the abomination of desolation.

Let no one deceive you by any means; for <u>that Day will not come unless</u> the falling away comes first, and <u>the man of sin is revealed, the son of perdition,</u> ⁴who opposes and exalts

---

44 There are many names given in Scripture for this person, but we will primarily refer to him as the "Antichrist" (1 John 2:18, 22; 4:3; 2 John 7).

himself above all that is called God or that is worshiped, so that <u>he sits as God in the temple of God, showing himself that he is God</u>. (2 Thess. 2:3–4)

D. The Drama of the Final Week

When we read Daniel 9 alongside Matthew 24 and 2 Thessalonians 2, we can conclude the following:

1. At some point in the future, a shrewd politician will successfully broker a peace treaty in the Middle East that will bring an end to centuries of hostility between Arabs and Israelis. People will rejoice in the peace and safety that this peace treaty brings to the region and the whole earth, but it is a false peace that will be cut short.

    For when they say, <u>"Peace and safety!"</u> then sudden destruction comes upon them, as labor pains upon a pregnant woman. And they shall not escape. (1 Thess. 5:3)

2. In the "middle of the week," or three and a half years into the peace treaty, the shrewd politician will declare himself to be God in the Jerusalem temple, end Jewish sacrifices, and demand worship. This detestable act will mark the beginning of the Great Tribulation. The second half of the "week," or the final three and a half years of this age, is the Great Tribulation, which will culminate with the return of Jesus, the salvation of Israel, and the destruction of the Antichrist.

    And then the lawless one [Antichrist] will be revealed, whom the Lord will consume with the breath of His mouth and <u>destroy</u> with the brightness of His coming. (2 Thess. 2:8)

    I was watching; and the same horn [Antichrist] was making war against the saints, and prevailing against them, ²²until the Ancient of Days came, and <u>a judgment was made in favor of the saints of the Most High</u>, and the time came for the saints to possess the kingdom. (Dan. 7:21–22)

    Seventy weeks are determined for your people and for your holy city, . . . to bring in everlasting righteousness, to seal up [fulfill] vision and prophecy. (Dan. 9:24)

E. The latter half of Daniel's seventieth week is described in the account of the Antichrist ("little horn") in Daniel 7, where it is referred to as a period lasting "a time and times and half a time." This is also the primary time period described in the book of Revelation, where it is expressed as "forty-two months," or "one thousand two hundred and sixty days." All three of these descriptions refer to the identical time frame, which is the final three and a half years before Jesus returns.

He [the Antichrist] shall speak pompous words against the Most High, shall persecute the saints of the Most High, and shall intend to change times and law. Then the saints shall be given into his hand <u>for a time and times and half a time.</u> (Dan. 7:25)

But leave out the court which is outside the temple, and do not measure it, for it has been given to the Gentiles. And <u>they will tread the holy city underfoot for forty-two months</u>. ³And I will give power to my two witnesses, and <u>they will prophesy one thousand two hundred and sixty days</u>, clothed in sackcloth. (Rev. 11:2–3)

F. In its simplest form, Daniel's seventieth week can be illustrated as follows:

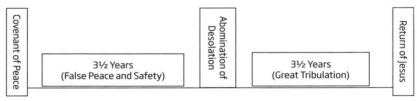

Daniel's Seventieth Week (Seven Years)

V. Primary People and Events of the Day of the Lord Drama

A. The Antichrist and the False Prophet

1. The Antichrist (Rev. 13:1–10) will be a world leader who wages war against God and His people. He will have the greatest political coalition, the largest army, the biggest worldwide religious network, and the most money and power of any man in history.

2. The False Prophet (13:11–18) is the Antichrist's primary associate and is the leader of the end-time, worldwide

religious network. He will be devoted to causing everyone on earth to worship Satan and the Antichrist (13:4, 8). He will use demonic miracles to deceive (13:12–14), political and military power to kill all who resist (13:15), and economic oppression to control the nations (13:16–17).

B. Babylon the Great

The great harlot Babylon (Rev. 17:1–18:24) will be a worldwide, demonic, economic, and religious network, probably based in the city of Babylon (located fifty miles south of Baghdad in modern-day Iraq). It will seduce many to do evil and persecute the saints during the first half of Daniel's seventieth week.

C. The Great Falling Away (Apostasy)

Great deception will arise within the Church in the end times. This deception will justify sinful behavior, and many believers will fall away from the faith out of love for sin (Matt. 24:12; 2 Thess. 2:3; 1 Tim. 4:1).

D. The Abomination of Desolation

This will occur when the Antichrist declares himself to be God by setting up his image, or idol, in the Jerusalem temple in the middle of Daniel's seventieth week (Dan. 8:13; 9:26–27; 11:31; 12:11; Matt. 24:15; Mark 13:14; 2 Thess. 2:3–4; Rev. 13:12–18). It will be an abomination to God because the Antichrist will demand to be worshiped as God, and many will fully respond to this demand. The desolation is twofold: those who do not worship the idol will be killed by the Antichrist, and, at His return, Jesus will bring an end to the Antichrist and his followers.

E. The Great Tribulation

1. The Great Tribulation is the term used by Jesus during His Olivet discourse (Matt. 24:21) to describe the second half of Daniel's seventieth week, after the Antichrist openly proclaims himself to be God in the temple (2 Thess. 2:4). It is also known as the time of "Jacob's trouble" (Jer. 30:7), or it is simply identified by its duration (Dan. 7:25; Rev. 11:2–3). During this period of time, great trouble will be released on the earth (particularly in and around the land

of Israel and against the Jewish people), and billions will be killed.

2. In the Great Tribulation pressure will come from four main factors:

    a. *God's wrath* against the rebellious.

    b. *Satan's rage* as he persecutes the saints through the Antichrist's reign of terror.

    c. *Man's sins* toward one another.

    d. *Creation's groan* through earthquakes, storms, and violent weather patterns.

3. God's judgment will be seen most clearly in the seven seals, seven trumpets, and seven bowls of wrath as described in Revelation 6:1–16:21. These constitute the core judgment activities of the Great Tribulation period that lasts for three and a half years, and end with the battle of Jerusalem and the second coming of Jesus (Rev. 19:11–21). There will be three different responses to God's judgments:

    a. Fear—Unbelievers will respond in fear (6:15–17), leading them to curse God (16:21) without repenting (9:20–21).

    b. Praise—Believers will glorify God for His power and salvation (Rev. 7:9–10; 11:13; 14:6–7).

    c. Prayer—Believers will also agree with Jesus through intercession, as He releases His judgments against the Antichrist's empire during the final three and a half years (Rev. 8:3–5).

4. The purpose of the Great Tribulation is to purify God's people through affliction (Dan 11:35; 12:10; Eph. 5:27; Rev. 19:7–8), release an ingathering of souls including the salvation of Israel, vindicate the saints, expose the apostate within the Church, and demonstrate God's power in protecting the saints (Rom. 9:17). It expresses God's justice in punishing sin (Isa. 26:21; 2 Thess. 1:6–10) and purges the earth before the millennial kingdom (Isa. 24:4–6; Zech. 13:2).

5. When considering the Great Tribulation, we must view it through God's principle of judgment: He uses the least severe means to reach the greatest number of people at the deepest level of love, without violating anyone's free will.

F. Glory of the Church during the Great Tribulation

1. During the Great Tribulation, the Lord will release great glory on His people related to protection, provision, prayer, prophecy, and revival. This grace and glory will protect sincere believers from falling away under the fierce influence and wrath of the Antichrist. A great example of supernatural protection of God's people is seen in the book of Exodus when God did not allow the plagues of Egypt to touch the place where His people dwelled. God will use this "Goshen principle"[45] at an even greater level in the coming days (Exod. 9:4–6, 26; 10:23; 11:7).

    I will set apart the land of Goshen, in which My people dwell, that no swarms of flies shall be there . . . ²³I will make a difference between My people and your people. (Exod. 8:22–23)

    Seek the LORD, all you meek of the earth . . . <u>it may be that you will be hidden</u> [protected] in the day of the LORD's anger [judgments]. (Zeph. 2:3)

2. Believers will not be protected from persecution at the hands of the Antichrist, yet multitudes of believers will come out of the Great Tribulation victorious through martyrdom (Dan. 7:21, 25; 8:24; 11:33–35; 12:7, 10; Rev. 6:9–11; 11:7; 12:11; 13:7, 15; 16:5–7; 17:6; 18:24; 19:2).

    These are the <u>ones who come out</u> [one by one] <u>of the great tribulation</u>, and washed their robes and made them white in the blood of the Lamb. (Rev. 7:14)

---

45 During the time of Moses and the plagues of Egypt, God did not allow His judgments to touch the place where His people lived, a place called Goshen (Exod. 8:22–23). Though the plagues were poured out in Egypt and all around the Israelites, nobody in Goshen was sick or affected, not even their livestock (9:4, 6, 26; 10:23; 11:7). This same "Goshen principle" will be seen in the end times as the mark, or seal of God, is put on the saints to protect them from the judgments of God (Ezek. 9:4–6; Rev. 7:2–3; 9:4).

It was <u>granted to him to make war with the saints</u> and <u>to overcome them</u>. And authority was given him over every tribe, tongue, and nation. (Rev. 13:7)

3.   The praying church will operate with great authority, strengthened by intimate friendship with God (Isa. 25:9; 27:2–5, 13; 30:18–19; 42:10–13; 62:6–7; Joel 2:12–17; Matt. 21:13; Luke 18:7–8; Rev. 5:8–10; 8:3–5; 22:17). Moreover, the Lord will release a prophetic spirit on the Church and all of God's people will prophesy (Isa. 26:9; Jer. 23:20; Dan. 11:33–35; Mal. 4:6; Matt. 17:11; Acts 2:17–18; Rev. 11:3–6; 18:20). The culmination of this prophetic activity will be the *two witnesses*, two prophets who will preach with great power for three-and-a-half years during the Great Tribulation (Rev. 11:3–6). Like Moses and Elijah, they will do great miracles (Exod. 5:1–12:30; 1 Kgs. 17:1; Mal. 4:5; Luke 4:25).

4.   There will be a great harvest of souls as the Lord releases the greatest revival and outpouring of the Spirit in history, and the Church will come to full maturity (Matt. 16:18; 24:14; John 17:21–26; Acts 2:17–21; Eph. 4:13; 5:26–27; Rev. 5:9; 14:6).

I looked, and behold, a <u>multitude</u> which no one could number <u>of all nations,</u> . . . [and] these are the ones who come out of the great tribulation. (Rev. 7:9, 14)

G.   The Second Coming Procession

Jesus' second coming, to establish His millennial kingdom, is the ultimate prophetic theme of the end times (Zech. 14:1–21; Matt. 24:1–51; Mark 13:1–37; Luke 21:1–38; Rev. 19:11–21). It will occur in three distinct stages:

1.   Jesus' procession over the entire earth in the sky to rapture the saints (Matt. 24:30–31; Rev. 1:7).

2.   Jesus' procession on the land traveling through Jordan to the Mount of Olives (Isa. 63:1–6; Hab. 3:3–18).

3.   Jesus' procession into Jerusalem from the Mount of Olives (Ps. 24:7–10; Zech. 14:4; Matt. 23:39).

H. The Rapture

The rapture of the Church will occur when Jesus comes upon the clouds in the sky and "catches up" all believers in the air. It will not be a secret event, but a dramatic one witnessed by believers and unbelievers alike (Rev. 1:7). It will occur in context to the second coming of Jesus (1 Thess. 4:13–5:11). The saints will be instantly changed as they receive resurrected bodies that radiate His glory.

Behold, I tell you a mystery: We shall not all sleep, but we shall all be changed—⁵²in a moment, in the twinkling of an eye, at the last trumpet. For the trumpet will sound, and the dead will be raised incorruptible, and we shall be changed. (1 Cor. 15:51–52)

I. The Battle of Jerusalem

The battle of Jerusalem is the final battle in a three-and-a-half-year military campaign by the Antichrist and his armies against Jerusalem. The campaign culminates at the return of Jesus to Jerusalem as He destroys the Antichrist, the False Prophet, and their armies (Joel 3:2–15; Zeph. 3:8; Zech. 14:1–5; Rev. 16:16; 19:11–21).

For I will gather all nations to battle against Jerusalem. (Zech. 14:2)

J. The Salvation of Israel

After judging Jerusalem, God will comfort her (Isa. 40:1–31) and give her salvation in exchange for her sin. All of Israel will be saved in one day, and their sins will be forgiven, as they are brought into the New Covenant through Jesus, the Messiah (Jer. 31:2; Zech. 3:9; 13:1–6). The entire nation refers to the remnant of Israel, which is the one-third who will survive the Great Tribulation (Zech. 13:8–9).

They will look on Me whom they have pierced [at the return of Jesus to Jerusalem]. . . . ¹¹In that day there shall be a great mourning in Jerusalem, . . . ¹²And the land shall mourn, every family by itself. (Zech. 12:10–12)

And so all Israel will be saved, as it is written: "The Deliverer will come out of Zion, and He will turn away ungodliness from Jacob." (Rom. 11:26)

K. The Millennial Kingdom

Jesus will rule the world from Jerusalem in perfect righteousness and continual peace, as He restores it to the conditions of the garden of Eden. His kingdom on earth will affect every sphere of life, including political, economic, educational, agricultural, environmental, family, media, arts, technology, athletics, and social spheres of life (Pss. 2:1–12; 110:1–7; Isa. 2:1–4; 9:6–7; 11:1–16; 51:1–8; 60:1–62:12; 65:17–25; Matt. 6:10; 17:11; 19:28; 28:19; Acts 3:21; Rev. 20:1–6).

Jerusalem shall be called the Throne of the LORD, and all the nations shall be gathered to it, to the name of the LORD, to Jerusalem. (Jer. 3:17)

SUMMARY

We have now concluded an overview of what Scripture reveals concerning the end times. This understanding of biblical revelation held by the International House of Prayer in Kansas City is commonly referred to as historic premillennialism, and has been shared by many throughout church history. As we have seen, this perspective includes the conviction that the Bible clearly teaches that the rapture will occur at the end of the Great Tribulation. Consequently, historic premillennialism can also be called the posttribulation view of the end times.

Because of our belief in a victorious church in the midst of the Great Tribulation, we also refer to the historic premillennial view as apostolic premillennialism. We use the term *apostolic* to refer to the vision, values, and victory of the New Testament church. Apostolic Christianity, or New Testament Christianity, will reemerge in the end times as the Spirit raises up a victorious church in unity, intimacy, and maturity (Rev. 22:17).

QUESTIONS

Reviewing (see answers on page 99)

A. The _____ of the _____ refers to the unusual end-time events related to the second coming of Jesus.

B. Understanding the sequence of events revealed in the book of _____ is critical to understanding the timing of the end-time events described in the book of Revelation and elsewhere in Scripture.

C. How long will the Great Tribulation last?

1. Seven years

2. Seventy weeks

3. Forty-two months

4. A time, times, and half a time

D. During the Great Tribulation, what is not a source of pressure?

1. The wrath of God on the rebellious.

2. The rage of Satan against the saints.

3. The renewal of the earth to an Eden-like paradise.

4. The actions of evil people against one another.

E. The rapture of the Church will not be a _____ event, but a _____ one witnessed by all believers and unbelievers.

Small Group Discussion

A. Given that the broad Day of the Lord covers over one thousand years, and not just a twenty-four hour period, why is that extended period still called the "Day" of the Lord (Joel 2:1, 11; Mal. 3:2; 4:5)? Why do you think God has chosen to use this specific phrase (Joel 3:14–17; Zech. 14:3–4; Matt. 24:8; 2 Pet. 3:7–8; Rev. 11:15–18)?

B. How can three and a half years of false peace and safety actually prepare the earth to receive the Antichrist (Dan. 9:27; 1 Thess. 5:3)? In the midst of the false peace and safety, what should the Church be praying and proclaiming (Joel 2:12–17; Matt. 24:4–44; John 14:6; Acts 3:19–21; Eph. 1:17–19; 3:14–21; Rev. 17:1–18:24)?

C. How will martyrdom in the Church actually work to strengthen believers and judge Satan and his kingdom (Gen. 4:10; John 12:24–25; 1 Cor. 1:21–29; Rev. 6:9–11; 12:11)?

D. Revelation 9 describes four demonic angels who are released to kill a third of mankind at a specific hour, day, month, and year. If there are clear, set times when events will occur at the end of the age, what does Peter mean when he says that believers can "hasten the day of God" (2 Pet. 3:12; cf. Joel 2:14)?

E. In the end times, believers will not be protected from persecution at the hands of the Antichrist. To prepare for those greater times of trouble, how can you learn to endure your lesser troubles today (Luke 11:13; John 14:26; Gal. 5:22–25; Heb. 12:1–15; Jas. 1:2–4; 4:7–10; 1 Pet. 1:6–9)?

FURTHER RESOURCES

Books

Bickle, Mike. *Omega: Leader's Tool Kit*. Kansas City, MO: Forerunner Publishing, 2006.

Miller, Stephen B. *Daniel*. New American Commentary, Vol. 18. Nashville, TN: Holman Reference, 1994.

Pawson, David. *When Jesus Returns.* London: Hodder and Stoughton, 1995.

Richardson, Joel. *The Islamic Antichrist: The Shocking Truth about the Real Nature of the Beast.* Los Angeles: WND Books, 2009.

Sliker, David. *Biblical Foundation of Eschatology Study Guide.* Kansas City, MO: Forerunner Books, 2008.

Walvoord, John. *Daniel: The Key to Prophetic Revelation.* Chicago: Moody Press, 1989.

Audio

Bickle, Mike. *End Times Questions & Answers Parts 1 and 2.* May 30, 2009. http://www.MikeBickle.org.

———. *Overview of the End Times Part 1.* July 2, 2005. http://www.MikeBickle.org.

———. *Overview of the End Times Part 2.* July 23, 2005. http://www.MikeBickle.org.

———. *Overview of the Millennial Kingdom: Heaven on Earth.* July 18, 2009. http://www.MikeBickle.org.

———. *Overview of the New Jerusalem: Motivation for Righteousness Part 1.* January 29, 2005. http://www.MikeBickle.org.

———. *Overview of the New Jerusalem: Motivation for Righteousness Part 2.* February 5, 2005. http://www.MikeBickle.org.

———. *Overview of the New Jerusalem: Motivation for Righteousness Part 3.* February 12, 2005. http://www.MikeBickle.org.

———. *Overview of the Seals, Trumpets, and Bowls.* December 1, 2007. http://www.MikeBickle.org.

Hood, Allen. *Life of Daniel (DVD series).* http://www.ihop.org/store.

5 Introduction to the Book of Revelation

INTRODUCTION

A group of seminary students used to play basketball in a local gym. Each week, a janitor would come to let them in when they arrived, and lock up when they left. While they were playing, he would sit on the bleachers reading his Bible. One day, one of the students was shocked to find that he was reading the book of Revelation. He wondered how a simple janitor could understand such a "difficult" book of the Bible, since many of his professors disagreed over the meaning of the book. Intrigued, he asked the janitor whether he understood what it meant. "Oh, yes!" said the janitor, "It means that Jesus is going to win!" For many people, the book of Revelation is avoided, either out of fear or because of its supposed "difficulty." In this lesson, we will look at the purpose and primary themes of this book. It is a manual to help every believer walk victoriously in the darkest hour of history.

TEACHING

I. **The Purpose of the Book of Revelation**

    A. The book of Revelation sets out in great detail God's action plan to take over the kingdoms of the earth through Jesus. It reveals the heart and leadership of Jesus at the end of the age like no other book in Scripture. Moreover, Revelation gives us more information on the end times than any other book in the Bible.

    B. Many people avoid reading the book of Revelation because they either do not understand it, or they are offended by the activity of Jesus as He releases judgments upon the earth. When rightly understood, however, this prophecy is designed to fill us with great hope and confidence. The Church will be victorious both, in the midst of the Great Tribulation and afterwards, as we rule and reign with Christ during His millennial kingdom.

    C. The content of the book of Revelation was not given to terrify us, confuse us, or stimulate centuries of academic debate. It is called the "Revelation of Jesus" (1:1) because it reveals His heart and brilliant leadership. Secondarily, it is a book about events in the end times, and gives us understanding of the great shakings that are going to be released upon the earth by Jesus at the very end of the age. The Father gave us this book to reveal the beauty of Jesus, and to help us prepare for all that is to come, so that we would endure until the end (2 Thess. 2:3).

D.   The book of Revelation is a "canonized" prayer manual to prepare the Church for the events of the end times. It is the end-time book of Acts, given to us in advance, so that we may walk in a unified prayer focus. Revelation is a record of the acts of the Spirit through the end-time apostles and prophets.

E.   As Moses released the plagues on Egypt through prayer in the book of Exodus, and as the first apostles released God's power through prayer in the book of Acts, the end-time judgments will be released in agreement through the praying church.

F.   The book of Revelation is focused on describing four things:

1.   The character and personality of Jesus as the heavenly Bridegroom, King, and Judge.

2.   God's action plan to take over the earth.

3.   The role of the Church in partnering with Jesus to release the judgments of God.

4.   The Church's necessary preparation to endure and overcome in the midst of great trouble.

G.   Studying the book of Revelation is essential for believers. It provides important information to prepare us to persevere through the greatest season of tribulation the Church has ever known.

H.   Revelation is unique in being the only book in the Bible in which God promises a special blessing to those who read, hear, and keep the words of the prophecy, as well as a curse to anyone who adds to or takes from it (Rev. 22:18–19). The primary way in which believers will be blessed is by being equipped to overcome in the darkest hour of human history.

***Blessed is he** who **reads** and those who **hear** the words of this prophecy, and **keep** those things which are written in it; for the time is near. (Rev. 1:3)*

I.   The book of Revelation does not picture the people of God escaping the Great Tribulation through a secret rapture. Nor does it picture the Church defeated by the devil or offended with the temporal judgments of Christ. In contrast, Revelation paints a picture of a glorious Bride who stands victorious in the midst of great trouble as she worships her heavenly Bridegroom.

J.   In the final years before Jesus returns, the Church will undergo unparalleled tribulation, which will be cut short by the return of Jesus (Matt. 24:22). The picture is not of a Bride that is simply enduring this trouble while she waits to be rescued by her heavenly Bridegroom. To the contrary, this time of great trouble is the Church's most glorious hour, in which she shines in bright righteousness and partners with the Lord, in releasing His judgments against unrighteousness (Rev. 5:8–10; 8:3–6; 15:2–8).

K.   The book of Revelation is a call for the Church to overcome in the midst of the darkest hour of human history. During this time, the rage of Satan, the wickedness of man, and the temporal judgments of God will be released on the earth in fullness.

L.   Revelation 1 spells out many truths about the majesty of Jesus that are meant to equip our hearts to overcome in times of great trouble. The letters to the seven churches in Revelation 2 and 3 focus on the issue of overcoming in the midst of persecution and divine delay. The remainder of the book contains critical information to help the Church make sense of circumstances, and stay faithful in the midst of the greatest time of trouble that the world has ever seen.

M.   The Lord will use this time of trouble to purify His Bride and cause her to shine with His glory and righteousness. The book of Revelation is the story of the ultimate triumph of the saints over all her enemies. At the end of the story, Jesus does not come to deliver a defeated, bedraggled Bride, but a people who have made themselves ready to meet their King.

Let us be glad and rejoice and give Him glory, for the marriage of the Lamb has come, and His wife has made herself ready. ⁸And to her it was granted to be arrayed in fine linen, clean and bright, for the fine linen is the righteous acts of the saints. (Rev. 19:7–8)

N. As we enter into understanding the message of Revelation, we will be empowered to overcome in the midst of tribulation, as God brings us into agreement with His plan and purpose. Those who overcome will be those who know their God and remain faithful to Him, despite the fierce assault of the enemy.

Those who do wickedly against the covenant he shall corrupt with flattery; but <u>the people who know their God shall be strong</u>, and carry out great exploits. ³³And those of the people who understand shall instruct many; yet for many days they shall fall by sword and flame, by captivity and plundering. (Dan. 11:32–33)

II. **The Revelation of Jesus as Bridegroom, King, and Judge**

A. The main purpose of the book of Revelation is to reveal the personality, power, and action plan of Jesus in preparing His Church to participate with Him in releasing God's glory in all the nations. Confidence in the love, authority, and power of Jesus is foundational to being prepared to partner with Him in the release of His purposes.

The <u>Revelation of Jesus Christ</u>, which God gave Him to show His servants. (Rev. 1:1)

B. The Father commissioned Jesus to reveal more of His majesty to His Church. In response, Jesus revealed Himself as the Bridegroom King, who judges all that hinders love as He takes over the earth.

1. Jesus is a passionate Bridegroom who is filled with tender, yet jealous love. He will come only in context to a prepared Bride who lives in unity with Him and the Spirit.

The marriage of the Lamb has come, and His wife has made herself ready. (Rev. 19:7)

2. Jesus is the King who will intervene to save the earth by taking over the governments of the nations, for the glory of God and the good of His people. He will replace all the unrighteous governments on earth with righteous leaders and laws.

The seventh angel sounded: and there were loud voices in heaven, saying, "The kingdoms of this world have become the kingdoms of our Lord . . . and He shall reign forever!" (Rev. 11:15)

3. Jesus is a righteous and wise Judge who works to confront all hatred of God, in order to establish love for Him across the whole earth (Rev. 16:5–7; 19:1–5).

    Great and marvelous are Your [Jesus'] works, . . . Just and true are Your ways, O King of the saints! . . . ⁴For Your judgments have been manifested. (Rev. 15:3–4)

C. There is no contradiction between Jesus as Bridegroom and Jesus as Judge. Jesus is filled with burning desire and fierce zeal to remove everything that hinders love, and His love is expressed and promoted by His redemptive judgments. The zealous Jesus of Armageddon, who slays the wicked, is the same Bridegroom God of love and tenderness who gathers His lambs in His arms, and carries them in His bosom (Isa. 40:11; Rev. 19:11–16).

D. Satan works to confuse the Church about the judgments of Jesus with the hope of *dividing* her over His leadership, and keeping her *unprepared* in prayer. His aim is to deceive believers so they will be *offended* at Jesus over His judgments, instead of trusting His perfect, loving leadership.

E. All heaven will rejoice as Jesus releases judgments against those who hate God and His salvation (Pss. 82:8; 94:1–17; Rev. 11:17–18; 15:3–4; 18:20–21).

    A great multitude in heaven, saying, "<u>Alleluia</u>! . . . ²For <u>true and righteous are His judgments</u>, because He has judged the great harlot . . ." ³Again they said, "<u>Alleluia</u>!" (Rev. 19:1–3)

F. As the saints rejoice at the love and truth of Jesus, unbelievers will hate and rage against Him (Ps. 2:1–3).

    The nations were <u>angry</u> and Your wrath has come. (Rev. 11:18)

G. The main battle at the end of the age is over the revelation of Jesus Christ. The Holy Spirit was sent to glorify and exalt Jesus by guiding us into all truth about Him (John 16:13–14). In the end times, some believers will give heed to doctrines that lie about the person of Jesus.

The Spirit <u>expressly says</u> that in <u>latter times</u> some will depart from the faith, <u>giving heed</u> to deceiving spirits and doctrines of demons, . . . ²having their conscience seared. (1 Tim. 4:1–2)

H. The great end-time conflict will center on defining who Jesus is. There are three key truths about Him that offend humans. First, He is God, and therefore can rightfully establish absolute standards by which He will judge the nations. Second, Jesus is the only way of salvation. Finally, He alone possesses the wisdom and love to judge sin in time and eternity. These truths are offensive because they make God the center of existence instead of man.

I. The most important issue to the early apostles concerned the identity of Jesus. As with the early church, the question to end-time leaders will be, "Who do you say that I am?" As we agree with the truth of who Jesus is, we are able to partner with Him through prayers that bind and loose in agreement with His Word.

He asked His disciples, saying, "<u>Who do men say that I</u>, the Son of Man, <u>am</u>?" ¹⁴They said, "Some say John the Baptist, some Elijah, and others Jeremiah . . ." ¹⁵He said, "<u>But who do you say that I am</u>?" ¹⁶Peter answered . . . "You are the <u>Christ</u>, the Son of the <u>living God</u>.". . . ¹⁸"On this rock I will <u>build My church</u>, and the gates of <u>Hades</u> shall <u>not prevail</u> against it. ¹⁹I will give you the <u>keys</u> of the kingdom . . . and <u>whatever you bind on earth</u> will be bound in heaven, and <u>whatever you loose on earth</u> will be loosed in heaven." (Matt. 16:13–19)

J. Jesus is fully God and fully man. In Revelation 1, we have one of the fullest pictures of Jesus as the God-man who is Bridegroom, King, and Judge. He will openly manifest His power to prepare His Bride, win the harvest, and cleanse and restore the earth.

K. The clearest picture of Jesus as our Bridegroom, King, and Judge is in Revelation 19:11–21. There is no contradiction between the revelation of Jesus in the Gospels and the revelation of Jesus in the book of the same name. The same Jesus who brings peace and goodwill to all who receive Him will confront all who aggressively resist and hate His leadership. It is His kindness that desires to free us from our sin and reveal His beauty to our hearts.

He [Jesus] . . . was called Faithful and True, and in righteousness He judges and makes war. . . . ¹³He was clothed with a <u>robe dipped in</u> blood, . . . ¹⁵out of His mouth goes a sharp sword, that with it He should <u>strike</u> the nations. He will rule them with a rod of iron. <u>He treads the winepress of the fierceness and wrath of Almighty God.</u> ¹⁶And on His robe and on His thigh a name written: KING OF KINGS AND LORD OF LORDS. (Rev. 19:11–16)

III. Three of the Central Themes in the Book of Revelation

The book of Revelation highlights three themes that are crucial for the end-time Church to understand: the coming kingdom of God, the tribulation that God's people will experience, and the importance of perseverance in the midst of negative circumstances.

I, John, your brother and fellow partaker in the <u>tribulation</u> and <u>kingdom</u> and <u>perseverance</u> which are in Jesus. (Rev. 1:9, NASB)

A. Kingdom

1. The book of Revelation is about the coming of God's kingdom to the earth in fullness. It is the story of how God is going to fully eradicate sin and wickedness from the earth and enforce His righteous rule over every nation. God's kingdom will culminate in the complete renewal of the heavens and the earth, and the joining together of all things in Christ (Eph. 1:10) as God makes the earth His eternal resting place (Rev. 21:3).

2. The book of Revelation gives us a glorious picture of the inheritance of the saints in God's kingdom and contrasts it with the ultimate destiny of the wicked. Becoming familiar with the hope of our calling (Eph. 1:18) is crucial to staying steady in the end times.

B. Tribulation

1. The book of Revelation is the revelation of Jesus as the righteous Judge of all the earth who is going to shake everything that can be shaken (Heb. 12:26–28).

2. The primary theme of the tribulation is God's judgment that is released by Jesus against the Antichrist's empire. The secondary theme is tribulation against the saints from the Antichrist (Rev. 12:12; 13:4, 7).

3. The book of Revelation describes the Church being acquainted with great suffering at the hands of the Antichrist and his world empire (Rev. 6:9; 7:14; 11:7; 12:11–12, 17; 13:7; 16:6; 17:6). In the midst of martyrdom and persecution, the Church will remain free from offense because they know their God and trust His leadership (Dan. 11:32; Rev. 14:4).

C. Perseverance

1. One of the goals of the book of Revelation is to call the Church to persevere and overcome in the midst of the greatest shaking the world has ever seen (1 John 5:4; Rev. 2:7, 11, 17, 26; 3:5, 12, 21; 17:14; 21:7).

2. The book of Revelation provides a glorious picture of the Church walking in partnership and victory with Jesus at the end of the age. Understanding both the ultimate victory of God's kingdom and the activity of Jesus in judgment is designed to give God's people grace to persevere in the midst of great trouble. Along with Paul, they will confidently say:

    I consider that the sufferings of this present time are <u>not worthy to be compared</u> with the glory, which shall be revealed in us. (Rom. 8:18)

IV. **Our Preparation to Overcome**

The book of Revelation is a gift to the Church to prepare us in advance of the great shakings. It is intended to:

A. Inform us that the Great Tribulation is part of God's end-time plan to purify the Church and bring her forth without spot or wrinkle (Rev. 2:10; 5:8–10; 6:9–11; 7:9–14; 12:11; 13:9–12; 14:12; 19:6–9).

    We ourselves boast of you among the churches of God for your patience and faith in <u>all your persecutions and tribulations that you endure</u>, ⁵which is manifest evidence of the righteous judgment of God, <u>that you may be counted</u>

worthy of the kingdom of God, for which you also suffer. *(2 Thess. 1:4–5)*

B. Encourage us that those who endure until the end will receive great rewards (Rev. 2:7, 10, 17, 26–29; 3:5, 11–12, 21).

> *He who overcomes shall inherit all things*, *and I will be his God and he shall be My son. (Rev. 21:7)*

C. Give us confidence that God is in control in the midst of suffering and martyrdom (Rev. 1:8, 10, 17–19; 2:8; 15:3–4; 16:5–6, 15; 19:1–20:15; 22:13, 20).

D. Grant us understanding of our permanent, heavenly citizenship and the greatness of rewards for those who endure and overcome (Phil. 3:7–21; Heb. 11:13–16).

V. The Central Role of the Prayer Movement in the Book of Revelation

The book of Revelation describes in detail two global worship movements—one true and one false—that will grow to fullness at the end of the age. Anyone who is called to be a part of the end-time prayer movement must become intimately acquainted with the ultimate prayer manual called the book of Revelation.

A. Satan is raising up a demonically-inspired prayer and worship movement under the leadership of the Antichrist and the False Prophet. This movement will release unprecedented demonic power and evil on the earth.

> *All who dwell on the earth will worship him* [Antichrist], *whose names have not been written in the Book of Life of the Lamb slain from the foundation of the world. (Rev. 13:8)*

> *Then I saw another beast [False Prophet] coming up out of the earth, and he had two horns like a lamb and spoke like a dragon.* [12] *And he . . . causes the earth and those who dwell in it to worship the first beast, whose deadly wound was healed.* [13] *He performs great signs, so that he even makes fire come down from heaven on the earth in the sight of men. (Rev. 13:11–13)*

B. The nations of the earth will be fascinated with the Antichrist's *personality, leadership,* and *power,* and many will come into agreement with who he is and what he says he is going to do. The Bible equates worship of the Beast with the worship of Satan himself.

And all the world marveled and followed the beast [Antichrist]. ⁴So they worshiped the dragon [Satan] who gave authority to the beast; and they worshiped the beast, saying, "Who is like the beast? [fascination] Who is able to make war with him? [exaltation of his power]" (Rev. 13:3–4)

C.   God is raising up His Church as a Holy Spirit-empowered prayer and worship movement that is His first line of defense against this demonic prayer movement. As the Church comes into agreement with who Jesus is and what He is going to do, the prayer and worship of the saints in the end times will release God's judgment against the Antichrist's world empire. It will be the most powerful and effective prayer and worship movement in history (Pss. 29:1–11; 149:1–9; Isa. 24:14–16; 26:8–9; 42:10–13; 62:6–7; Joel 2:12–17, 32; Zeph. 2:1–3; Rev. 5:8; 8:4; 22:17).

And __shall God not avenge__ [grant justice and release judgment on behalf of] __His own elect__ who __cry out day and night to Him__, though He bears long with them? ⁸I tell you that __He will avenge them speedily__. (Luke 18:7–8)

D.   In the book of Revelation, John describes the end-time prayer movement in detail, with particular focus on the content and impact of the prayers and songs of the saints at the end of the age (Rev. 5:9–13; 7:9–12; 15:3–4). It is the ultimate prayer manual, designed to equip the saints to enter into their primary end-time identity as a prayer movement, without drawing back in fear.

E.   The final and ultimate description of the Church in the book of Revelation is the Bride of Christ, praying in unity with and under the anointing of the Holy Spirit.

And __the Spirit__ and __the bride__ say, __"Come!"__. . . ²⁰He [Jesus] who testifies to these things says, "Surely I am coming quickly." Amen. __Even so, come, Lord Jesus!__ (Rev. 22:17, 20)

F.   As the Church enters into her bridal identity, the prophetic singers and musicians will lead an anointed cry for her Bridegroom to return (Ps. 149:6–9; Isa. 42:10–12; Rev. 5:9–10; 15:3–4). There will be a crescendo of prayer and worship on the earth in concert with the prayer and worship in heaven. This movement will release God's judgments against His enemies and inaugurate the millennial kingdom.

SUMMARY

If the book of Revelation is truly the end-time book of Acts, then what does that mean for us? If it is truly the book of Exodus and the book of Acts combined and multiplied on a global level, then how will it impact our lives? To find the answer to these questions, we must pursue the heart of the Lord in prayer, fasting, study, and humility. While the best days are yet ahead for the Church, it is also our hour of greatest trial, with unprecedented measures of persecution and martyrdom. In light of this, let your hearts be filled with hope and trembling as the "great and terrible Day of the Lord" quickly approaches.

QUESTIONS

Reviewing (see answers on page 99)

A. Which of the following is the book of Revelation focused on describing?

1. The character and personality of Jesus as the Savior, Healer, and Provider.

2. God's action plan to remove the earth.

3. The role of the Church in partnering with Jesus to release the judgments of God.

4. The necessary preparation to endure and overcome in the midst of great trouble.

B. The book of Revelation is a "canonized" _____ _____ to prepare the Church for the events of the end times.

C. There is no contradiction between Jesus as _____ and _____.

D. The three central themes in the book of Revelation are:

1. Kingdom

2. Justification

3. Tribulation

4. Perseverance

E. The book of Revelation describes in detail two _____
_____ movements that will grow to fullness at the end
of the age.

Small Group Discussion

A. Why will the nations hate Jesus and rage against Him in the
end times (Ps. 2:1–3; Zech. 14:1–3; Rom. 1:18–25; 2 Thess. 2:7;
Rev. 11:18; 19:19; 20:7–9)?

B. Since the conflict in the end times will center on who Jesus is
(Matt. 16:13–19; John 16:13–14; 1 Tim. 4:1–2), what can you do
to solidify the truths of His divinity, humanity, and personality in your own heart and mind (Ps. 27:4; Luke 10:38–42; Rom.
10:8–11; Eph. 1:17–19; Col. 3:16; Rev. 1:3)?

C. What are some practical ways that you can read the book of
Revelation as an unveiling of the beauty and brilliant leadership of Jesus, rather than a book primarily about events (Ps.
119:18; John 5:39–40; 16:13–15; Eph. 1:17–19; Rev. 1:1–18)? What
are some questions you can ask as you read it?

D. How can the Lord's love be manifested in killing multitudes of His enemies at Armageddon (Prov. 6:34; Zech. 8:2; 2 Thess. 2:8–12; Heb. 12:26–27; Rev. 19:2, 11–16)?

E. If our final and ultimate description in the book of Revelation is as the Bride of Christ crying, "Come, Jesus" in unity with the Holy Spirit (Rev. 22:17, 20), how can we begin to walk in this identity now (Song 8:6–7; Matt. 22:37–39; John 15:9; 1 Cor. 2:9–10; 6:17; Eph. 1:17–19; 4:11–13; 5:25–32; Rev. 19:7)?

FURTHER RESOURCES

Books

Bickle, Mike. *Book of Revelation Study Guide.* Kansas City, MO: Forerunner Books, 2009.

Hayford, Jack. *E-Quake: A New Approach to Understanding the End Times Mysteries in the Book of Revelation.* Nashville, TN: Thomas Nelson, 1999.

Juster, Dan. *Revelation: The Passover Key.* Shippensburg, PA: Destiny Image, 1991.

Pawson, David. *Come with Me through Revelation.* Bristol, England: Terra Nova Publications, 2008.

Articles

Bickle, Mike. *Outline of the Book of Revelation.* http://www.MikeBickle.org.

———. *Role of Prayer in Revelation and the End Time Church.* http://www.MikeBickle.org.

———. *Where is the Church in the Book of Revelation?* http://www.MikeBickle.org.

Audio

Bickle, Mike. *A Simple Outline of the Book of Revelation.* June 27, 2009. http://www.MikeBickle.org.

————. *The End-Time Church Fully Engaged with the Holy Spirit.* September 23, 2005. http://www.MikeBickle.org.

————. *The King of Kings is Coming to Rule the Whole Earth.* February 19, 2005. http://www.MikeBickle.org.

6 Overview of the Book of Revelation

INTRODUCTION

Why is it so important to have directions when assembling furniture or appliances? The directions show you what the various parts are, where each piece goes, and how it all fits together. With this information that beautiful chair, desk, or stereo system can be properly built and used. In the same way, if you know what the various parts of the book of Revelation are and how they fit together, then you will be able to properly read, interpret, and apply it to your life. In this lesson, you will receive an overview of the book of Revelation as well as a general explanation of the various sections and parts of the prophecy.

TEACHING

I.   **Outline of the Book of Revelation: Four Main Parts**

   A.   Part One: John's Commission to Prophesy about the End Times (Rev. 1:1–20)

      1.   The book is called, "The Revelation of Jesus Christ," because it reveals His heart, power, and leadership in preparing the nations for God's glory.

      2.   The Father's primary purpose in giving us this book is to reveal the beauty of Jesus. Secondarily, it is a book about events in the end times.

   B.   Part Two: Seven Letters to the Seven Churches (Rev. 2:1–3:22)

      1.   Jesus spoke prophetically to seven first-century churches and called them to overcome. Though He addressed seven literal, historical churches in Asia Minor, the issues addressed will also be the most challenging for the end-time church.

      2.   The seven prophetic messages of Jesus are intended to give us instruction on how to best prepare for His coming, and can be summed up in the acrostic P.E.R.F.E.C.T.

         a.   Pursue Your First Love (2:1–7)

         b.   Endure Suffering (2:8–11)

        c.   **Resist False Teaching** (2:12–17)

        d.   **Flee Immorality** (2:18–29)

        e.   **Embrace Whole-heartedness** (3:1–6)

        f.   **Continue in Faithfulness** (3:7–13)

        g.   **Turn from Lukewarmness** (3:14–22)

C.   Part Three: Jesus Takes the Scroll (Rev. 4:1–5:14)

    1.   Jesus is commissioned by the Father to cleanse the earth, replace all evil governments, and drive the usurper off the earth.

    2.   The scroll represents the title deed of the earth and the action plan to judge, cleanse, and prepare the nations for the reign of Jesus, and bring the Church into maturity and unity with redeemed Israel.

D.   Part Four: The Battle Plan of Jesus (Rev. 6:1–22:21)

    1.   The chapters in this fourth part focus on the time of the Great Tribulation as God's judgments are loosed against the Antichrist's empire (Rev. 6:1–19:21) in a three-part series of twenty-one judgments (seven seals, seven trumpets, and seven bowls of wrath).

    2.   The end-time judgments are literal (actual events not to be explained away symbolically), future (their greatest fulfillment is future), progressive (increasing in intensity), and numbered (released in a sequential order).

II. The Battle Plan (Rev. 6:1–22:21)

A.   The main story line is contained in the fourth part of the book, and it can be summed up very simply in two parts: 1) things are going to get much worse for people on the earth before they get much better, and 2) things are going to get much better after they get much worse.

B.   The story line of the book unfolds in a chronological sequence so that the three numbered judgment series' unfold one after another. It will climax in the return of Jesus to set up His millennial kingdom from Jerusalem and culminate in the new heavens and the new earth. It is possible to identify five chronological sections in the book.

C. After each chronological section, the story line of the book is "paused," and an explanation is given to John by the angel who is with him (Rev. 1:1) to help him make sense of the activity in the previous section of the story. These five "angelic" explanations are interpretative sections of Revelation that answer two main questions. First, "Why are these judgments so severe?" Second, "What will happen to the Church during the Great Tribulation?"

D. Understanding the relationship between the chronological sections and the angelic explanations makes the book of Revelation much easier to grasp. As we become familiar with the symbolism of the angelic explanations, we will have confidence and zeal to go deeper in our study of the book.

III. Seven Primary Symbols in the Book of Revelation

A. Revelation is to be interpreted by its plain, face-value meaning. The events and numbers in Revelation are to be understood literally, unless Scripture specifically indicates that they are symbolic (Rev. 1:20; 5:6; 11:8; 12:1, 3, 9; 17:7, 9). Most of the time, the explanation of the symbols is given in the immediate context of the text or in other biblical passages. On rare occasions, the symbols are not explained in Scripture, but they are very straightforward and easy to understand in their historical, cultural context, according to the book's recipients. The challenge for us is simply that the context is unfamiliar.

B. Some of the symbols used by John are the same as those used by the prophet Daniel (Dan. 7:3–7, 12, 17; 8:4). Daniel prophesied of the Antichrist as the Beast with an evil empire (Dan. 7:7, 11, 19, 20–23) that was supported by ten kings seen as ten horns (Dan. 2:41–42; 7:7, 20, 24; cf. Rev. 12:3; 13:1; 17:3, 7, 12, 16).

C. The *Dragon* is always symbolic of Satan (Rev. 12:3, 4, 7, 9, 13, 16, 17; 13:2, 4; 16:13; 20:2).

D. The *Beast* is symbolic of the Antichrist (Rev. 13; 14:9–11; 17:3–17; 19:19–20; 20:4, 10). The Antichrist is called the *Beast* thirty-six times in Revelation. He will demand worldwide worship by requiring all who want to buy and sell to receive his mark. This economic and religious system will be facilitated by the False Prophet.

> *He [False Prophet] causes all, both small and great, rich and poor, free and slave, to receive a mark on their right hand or on their foreheads, ¹⁷and that <u>no one may buy or sell except one who has the mark or the name of the beast, or the number of his name</u>. (Rev. 13:16–17)*

E.   *Another beast* is symbolic of the False Prophet who is only called *another beast* once. Each other time he is called the *False Prophet* (Rev. 13:11–17; 16:13; 19:20; 20:10). Together, the Dragon, the Beast, and the False Prophet form an "unholy trinity."

F.   *Babylon* is a literal city that will probably be rebuilt on the river Euphrates in modern-day Iraq. It will function as the global center of demonic religious and economic networks (Isa. 13:1–14:32; 21:1–17; Jer. 50:1–51:64; Rev. 17:1–18:24), and it will seduce many to sin and persecute the saints.

G.   The *seven heads* are seven empires from history that persecuted Israel: Egypt, Assyria, Babylon, Persia, Greece, Rome, and the future, revived Roman Empire (Dan. 2:41–42; 7:7; Rev. 12:3; 13:1; 17:3–6).

H.   The *ten horns* speak of a future, ten-nation confederation of ten kings that will rule simultaneously over their own nations as they come into an enthusiastic partnership under the Antichrist's authority (Dan. 2:41–42; 7:7, 20, 24; 11:36–45; Rev. 12:3; 13:1; 17:3, 7, 12, 16).

I.   The *woman with the male-child* (Jesus) is the faithful remnant of Israel throughout history (Rev. 12:1–5). Satan will war with her offspring who are Gentile believers (Rev. 12:17).

IV.   **Chronological Section #1: Seven Seal Judgments (Rev. 6:1–17)**

A.   The seven seals are released by Jesus, the Lamb of God (Rev. 5:5; 6:1, 3, 5, 7, 9, 12; 8:1).

> *I saw when the <u>Lamb opened</u> one of the seals. (Rev. 6:1)*

B.   The seal judgments target the kingdom of darkness. God lifts His restraining hand off of evil men so that they attack one another with great hatred, and destroy one another's resources. The restraints upon man's sin are lifted, so the truth of his wickedness and lawlessness is seen. The fifth and sixth seals open the heavens to release God's power (Rev. 6:9–17).

C.   The Seven Seals (Rev. 6:1–17; 8:1)

    1.   White Horse: Antichrist's Political Aggression (Rev. 6:1–2)

    2.   Red Horse: Bloodshed and World War (Rev. 6:3–4)

    3.   Black Horse: Famine and Economic Crisis (Rev. 6:5–6)

    4.   Pale Horse: Disease and Death over One-Fourth of the Earth (Rev. 6:7–8)

    5.   Prayer Movement: Strengthened by the Prayers of the Martyrs (Rev. 6:9–11)

    6.   Cosmic Disturbances: Fear (Rev. 6:12–17)

    7.   Anointed Prayer: The Prayer Movement Releases the Judgments of Revelation 8:1–9:21

V.   **Angelic Explanation #1: Who Can Stand? (Rev. 7:1–17)**

For the great day of His wrath has come, and <u>who is able to stand</u>? (Rev. 6:17)

"Do not harm the earth, the sea, or the trees till we have <u>sealed</u> the servants of our God on their foreheads." ⁴I heard the number of those who were sealed: <u>144,000 of all the tribes of</u> . . . Israel were sealed . . . ⁹Behold, a <u>great multitude</u> . . . <u>of all nations</u> . . . before the throne . . . clothed with white robes . . . ¹⁰saying, "Salvation belongs to our God." (Rev. 7:3–4, 9–10)

A.   This angelic explanation answers the question: "Who can stand in the midst of so much pressure?" John sees a divine sealing that gives people physical and spiritual protection (Rev. 7:1–17). In particular, there will be 144,000 Jews who are sealed by God, physically protecting them before He strikes the earth to judge the Antichrist (Ezek. 9:6; Rev. 7:1–8). Gentile believers will also be sealed by God (Ps. 91:1–16; Rev. 9:4).

B.   There is a key principle at work in God's sealing: the saints are not to be subject to the wrath of God. He will protect them from His judgments, although not from the rage of Satan or persecution at the hands of man.

> For <u>*God did not appoint us to wrath,*</u> *but to obtain salvation through our Lord Jesus Christ,* [10]*who died for us, that whether we wake or sleep, we should live together with Him.* [11]<u>*Therefore comfort each other and edify one another,*</u> *just as you also are doing. (1 Thess. 5:9–11)*

C. At the time of the exodus from Egypt, Israel received a protective mark on their doors that saved their firstborn from death (Exod. 11:4–12:30). They were also protected from the other plagues that affected the Egyptians (Exod. 8:22–23; 9:4, 6, 26; 10:22–23).

D. The saints are not to fear that they will compromise under pressure of persecution because Gentile believers from every tribe, tongue, people, and nation are seen standing without wavering under persecution (Rev. 7:9–17). God promises that He will not allow His people to be tempted beyond what they are able, but with every temptation He will provide the way to overcome (1 Cor. 10:13).

VI. Chronological Section #2: First Six Trumpet Judgments (Rev. 8:2–9:21)

A. The trumpet judgments are supernatural acts of God to destroy the Antichrist's resources. They are released through nature (first four trumpets) and demons (fifth and sixth trumpets).

1. Food Supply: Burning One-Third of the Earth's Vegetation (8:7)

2. Food Supply: Destroying One-Third of the Sea (8:8–9)

3. Water Supply: Poisoning One-Third of the Earth's Fresh Water (8:10–11)

4. Light and Energy: Darkening One-Third of the Earth's Light (8:12)

5. Torment: Demonic Locusts that Torment for Five Months (9:1–12)

6. Death: Demonic Horsemen that Kill One-Third of the Earth (9:13–21)

B. The ten plagues of Egypt (Exod. 7:1–12:30) are prophetic types which foreshadow the global end-time plagues seen in the trumpet and bowl judgments. The first six trumpets parallel six of the plagues of Egypt:

1. The first trumpet parallels the seventh plague of hail and fire mingled with blood (Exod. 9:22–26).

2. The second and third trumpets parallel the first plague of the Nile turning to blood (Exod. 7:19–25).

3. The fourth trumpet parallels the ninth plague of darkness (Exod. 10:21–23).

4. The fifth trumpet parallels the eighth plague of locusts (Exod. 10:12–20).

5. The sixth trumpet parallels the tenth plague of death (Exod. 12:29–30).

C. The judgments of Revelation are an end-time application of the Egyptian plagues so as to prepare the saints for a final exodus from this present, evil age to the new kingdom order.

VII. Angelic Explanation #2: Prophetic Direction (Rev. 10:1–11:13)

A. This section is focused on the welfare of the saints, for God promises to provide prophetic direction and power to His people by releasing an unprecedented outpouring of the Holy Spirit (Acts 2:17–21).

B. God has concealed key prophetic information that will be revealed in the end times. This information will be disclosed at the perfect time to bring strength, protection, and direction to the saints.

1. God will reveal it to the Church (Rev. 10:7) and will bring forth prophetic messengers to declare mysteries concerning the end times that have been sealed until the time of the end.

    But you, Daniel, shut up the words, and <u>seal the book until</u> the time of the end. (Dan. 12:4)

2. God will release two prophetic witnesses who will help God's people with great power during the last three and a half years of the tribulation (Rev. 11:3–13).

VIII. Chronological Section #3: Second Coming and Rapture (Rev. 11:14–19)

Then the seventh angel sounded: and there were loud voices in heaven, saying, "<u>The kingdoms of this world have become the kingdoms of our Lord and of His Christ</u>, and He shall reign forever and ever! . . . ¹⁸<u>The nations were angry</u>, and <u>Your wrath has come</u>, and <u>the time of the dead, that they should be judged</u>, and that <u>You should reward Your servants</u> the prophets and the saints, and those who fear Your name, small and great, and <u>should destroy those who destroy the earth</u>." (Rev. 11:15, 18)

A. The second coming is not an instant event, but rather a three-stage procession that begins with the rapture at the seventh (last) trumpet (1 Cor. 15:52; Rev. 11:15).

And He will send His angels <u>with a great sound of a trumpet</u>, and they will gather together His elect from the four winds, from one end of heaven to the other. (Matt. 24:31)

For <u>the Lord Himself will descend from heaven</u> with a shout, with the voice of an archangel, and <u>with the trumpet of God</u>. And <u>the dead in Christ will rise first</u>. ¹⁷<u>Then we who are alive and remain shall be caught up together</u> with them in the clouds to meet the Lord in the air. And thus we shall always be with the Lord. ¹⁸Therefore <u>comfort one another with these words</u>. (1 Thess. 4:16–18)

B. The rapture is the first event in the three stages of the second coming procession:

1. Jesus comes across the earth in the sky to rapture the saints (Matt. 24:30–31; Rev. 1:7).

2. He comes across the land through Edom, which is modern-day Jordan (Isa. 63:1–6; Hab. 3:3–16).

3. The Lord enters Jerusalem as the King of kings (Matt. 23:39).

C. It is possible that the second coming procession occurs over the thirty-day period following the 1,260 days of the Great Tribulation, which is alluded to in Daniel 12.

And from the time that the daily sacrifice is taken away, and the abomination of desolation is set up, there shall be

one thousand two hundred and <u>ninety</u> days *[i.e. thirty days longer than the 1,260 days of the Great Tribulation].* **(Dan. 12:11)**

D. John highlights five things in his description of the seventh trumpet:

1. The kingdoms of the earth have come under the manifest leadership of Jesus.

2. The nations are enraged at Jesus.

3. The unrighteous dead will be judged.

4. The saints will be rewarded (Isa. 40:10; 62:11; Rev. 11:18; 19:7–8; 22:12).

5. The rebellious still on earth will be destroyed (Rev. 16:1–21).

IX. Angelic Explanation #3: Antichrist's Violent Confrontation (Rev. 12:1–14:20)

A. This angelic explanation occurs just after the announcement of the return of Jesus to take over all the kingdoms on the earth (Rev. 11:15). It explains why God's severe wrath requires all the governments on the earth to be replaced.

B. The Antichrist, and the nations in agreement with his leadership, violently confront God and His leadership (Ps. 2:1–12). This rage against God culminates in the Antichrist's war against God and His people under the direct influence of Satan, who will be cast to the earth (Rev. 12:1–17).

C. Revelation 13 describes the Antichrist waging war against God and His people with a political, military, and economic alliance. Furthermore, the False Prophet will be devoted to causing all nations to worship Satan and the Antichrist (Rev. 13:4, 8).

X. Chronological Section #4: Seven Bowl Judgments (Rev. 15:1–16:21)

A. The seven bowls of wrath are the third and final numbered series of judgments (Rev. 16:1–21). Jesus will destroy the infrastructure of the Antichrist's empire.

> *I [Father] will give You [Jesus] the nations for Your inheritance,
> . . . ⁹You shall break them with a rod of iron; You shall <u>dash
> them to pieces</u> like a potter's vessel. (Ps. 2:8–9)*

B. All the bowls will be poured out in context to the return of Jesus. This will culminate as He marches up through Jordan to fight the final battle of the "Armageddon campaign" in Jerusalem, and rescue the unsaved remnant of Israel (Isa. 63:1–6; Hab. 3:3–16; Zech. 12:1–9; 14:1–5).

C. The seven bowls of wrath (third judgment series) recall the ten plagues of Egypt (Exod. 7:1–12:30):

1. Sores: Painful Sores on Those Who Worship the Antichrist (Rev. 16:1–2)

2. Food Supply: Destroying the Sea with Blood and Killing All in It (Rev. 16:3)

3. Water Supply: Poisoning the Earth's Fresh Water with Blood (Rev. 16:4–7)

4. Torment: Scorching Heat and Fire from the Sun (Rev. 16:8–9)

5. Destruction: Darkness on the Antichrist's Global Empire (Rev. 16:10–11)

6. Global Guilt: Nations Deceived to Come to Armageddon (Rev. 16:12–16)

7. Annihilation: Shaking by Earthquakes and Hail Stones (Rev. 16:17–21)

XI. Angelic Explanation #4: Seduction by Babylon (Rev. 17:1–19:10)

A. The seventh bowl releases God's fierce judgment on Babylon (Rev. 16:19). The seduction of Babylon's wealth and immorality will permeate and infiltrate all the structures of society, requiring that she be destroyed.

B. The harlot will be a false counterfeit justice movement that unifies multitudes from the largest religions on the earth. Though she will appear to be great as she gives unprecedented humanitarian service to the poor, she is actually filled with immoral power and demonic motives. She will persecute and kill the saints as she seduces people to leave their belief systems and religious heritage. When this deceptive system has fulfilled its purpose, the Antichrist, with ten supporting kings, will destroy the Harlot Babylon religion and require everyone to worship him exclusively.

C. As a result of her seductive power and cruel persecution of the saints, God will judge the harlot in two stages. He will judge the religious network at the beginning of the Great Tribulation at the hands of ten kings (Rev. 17:16). Then, He will judge the economic network at the end of the Great Tribulation as Jesus releases His bowls of wrath upon her (Rev. 18:8).

XII. Chronological Section #5: Jesus' Triumphal Entry (Rev. 19:11–21:8)

Behold, a white horse. And He [Jesus] who sat on him was called Faithful and True, and in righteousness <u>He judges and makes war</u>. . . . ¹⁴And the armies in heaven . . . followed Him on white horses. ¹⁵Out of His mouth goes a sharp sword, that with it He should <u>strike the nations</u>. And He Himself will <u>rule</u> them . . . ¹⁶He has on His robe and on His thigh a name written: KING OF KINGS AND LORD OF LORDS. . . . ²⁰The beast [Antichrist] was captured, and with him the false prophet . . . These two were <u>cast alive into the lake of fire</u> burning with brimstone. ²¹And the rest were killed with the sword which proceeded from the mouth of Him who sat on the horse. (Rev. 19:11–21)

A. Revelation 19:11–21:8 describes the triumphal entry of Jesus into Jerusalem as King. He will be welcomed by the Jewish leadership of Jerusalem (Zech. 12:10; Matt. 23:39) and reign from David's throne over the newly saved nation of Israel (Rom. 11:26). As King of kings, His political rule will extend to the ends of the earth.

B. At the battle of Jerusalem, Jesus will destroy the armies of the Antichrist and throw the Antichrist and False Prophet into the lake of fire (Rev. 19:20). He will cast Satan into prison (Rev. 20:1–3) and establish His one-thousand-year rule, known as the millennial kingdom (Rev. 20:4–10). After the Millennium, all unbelievers will be judged before the great white throne

(Rev. 20:11–15), and the age to come will begin as God comes to dwell with man on the new earth (Rev. 21:3).

XIII. **Angelic Explanation #5: Restoration of All Things (Rev. 21:9–22:5)**

A. The final angelic explanation shows the victory of the Bride and describes the relationship between the millennial earth and the New Jerusalem (Rev. 21:9–22:5). God shows how He will vindicate and reward the saints for remaining faithful throughout the Great Tribulation. He also describes life in the New Jerusalem.

B. The New Jerusalem has been prepared as the place where all the saints will live forever in God's immediate presence (Heb. 11:10, 16; 12:22–24). During the Millennium, Jesus begins the process of bringing the heavenly and earthly realms together (Eph. 1:9–10). When the New Jerusalem comes to the earth, heaven will literally be on earth.

*The **New Jerusalem**, which **comes down** out of heaven from My God. (Rev. 3:12)*

C. During the millennial kingdom, the New Jerusalem will be connected to the millennial Jerusalem, creating a vast "governmental complex." It will be the governmental center of heaven and earth, referred to as Jesus' throne of glory (Matt. 19:28). The saints will easily travel from the New Jerusalem to the millennial earth as angels now travel from heaven to earth.

*When the Son of Man comes . . . then He will sit on the **throne of His glory**. (Matt. 25:31)*

SUMMARY

By knowing the four main parts, five chronological sections, five angelic sections, and seven main symbols of the book of Revelation, you are equipped to dive into this fascinating book and begin to understand its truth. In one of Jesus' final statements, He exhorts, "Blessed is he who keeps the words of the prophecy in this book" (Rev. 22:7). To "keep the words" means to attend, watch over, and guard this book in your heart. Now that you can learn what Revelation says, you are encouraged to remember what you learn. Remind yourself constantly of the truths of this book, and ask the Holy Spirit for revelation on how to apply them. These words will be a priceless blessing in your life, day after day.

QUESTIONS

Reviewing (see answers on page 100)

A. The Father's primary purpose in giving us the book of Revelation is to reveal the _____ of Jesus; and it is secondarily a book about _____ in the end times.

B. The end-time judgments in the book of Revelation are _____ (actual events not to be explained away symbolically), _____ (their greatest fulfillment is still to come), _____ (increasing in intensity), and _____ (released in sequential order).

C. The book of Revelation contains the following:

    1. Four main parts

    2. Five chronological sections

    3. Four angelic explanations

    4. Seven primary symbols

D. The seven seals are released by _____.

E. The judgments of Revelation are an end-time application of the Egyptian _____ to prepare the saints for a final _____ from this present evil age to the new kingdom order.

Small Group Discussion

A. Jesus gave John seven messages to seven churches in Asia that addressed specific issues, successes, and failures (Rev. 2:1–3:22). All seven of these messages are still relevant in the Body of Christ today, but which one of the seven do you think most pertains to the church of your nation, presently? What advice did Jesus give to overcome in this area, and what promise of reward does He give if you do?

B. Why do you think that Jesus gave His revelation to John with breaks between chronological events and angelic explanations? Why did He not just unveil the vision straight through?

C. Why do you think symbols are used in the five parenthetical sections? Why not use speech that would be immediately understood (Prov. 25:2; Matt. 11:25; 13:34–35; Luke 10:21)?

D. Why is the majority of the book of Revelation focused on God's wrath being poured out on the earth in the three series' of numbered judgments (Rev. 6:1–16:21)?

E. Why do you think Jesus will release His judgments in three different waves with seals (Rev. 6:1–17; 8:1), then trumpets (Rev. 8:2–9:21), then bowls (Rev. 15:1–16:21)? Why will He not just release them all at once (Exod. 7:14–12:30; Ezek. 33:11; 2 Pet. 3:9)?

FURTHER RESOURCES

Books

Ladd, George Eldon. *A Commentary on the Revelation of John.* Grand Rapids, MI: Wm. B. Eerdmans, 1972.

Thomas, Robert L. *Revelation 1–7: An Exegetical Commentary.* Chicago: Moody, 1992.

Thomas, Robert L. *Revelation 8–22: An Exegetical Commentary.* Chicago: Moody, 1995.

Walvoord, John. *The Revelation of Jesus Christ.* Chicago: Moody, 1989.

Audio

Bickle, Mike. *The Book of Revelation (Series).* http://www.MikeBickle.org.

———. *Seals, Trumpets, and Bowls: Studies in the Book of Revelation (Series).* http://www.MikeBickle.org.

———. *The Seven Churches of Revelation (Series).* http://www.MikeBickle.org.

———. *Studies in the Millennial Kingdom: Heaven on Earth (Series).* http://www.MikeBickle.org.

Pawson, David. *Book of Revelation Seminar (Series).* http://www.ihop.org/store.

Answer Key

Lesson 1: Why Should We Study the End Times?

A. The subject of eschatology is the most <u>discussed</u> subject in Scripture, yet it is the least <u>understood</u> subject in the Bible.

B. Which of the following is true:

　　1. The Church will be raptured before the Great Tribulation.

　　2. <u>The Church will go through the Great Tribulation.</u>

　　3. The Great Tribulation represents trials experienced throughout church history.

　　4. The Church will be raptured at the abomination of desolation.

C. True: Unless the Bible says it is symbolic, it means what it says and says what it means.

D. Not understanding God's ways will cause our hearts to draw back in <u>offense</u> and <u>anger</u> at God as the events of the end times unfold.

E. Studying the end times causes us to be fascinated with Jesus because it is a study of His <u>glory</u>, His <u>leadership</u>, and His <u>ways</u>.

Lesson 2: Can We Know the Generation of the Lord's Return?

A. True—It is possible to know the generation in which the Lord returns.

B. Which of the following were signs for Noah's generation that a cataclysmic, worldwide judgment was coming?

　　1. <u>The death of Noah's grandfather, Methuselah.</u>

　　2. The gradual increase of rainstorms throughout Noah's lifetime.

　　3. <u>Noah's building of the ark.</u>

　　4. <u>God's word to Noah about sending rain in seven days.</u>

C. Much of the Old Testament was written with a <u>future</u> or <u>eschatological</u> fulfillment in view.

D. Jesus said there would be one generation in history in which the <u>wheat</u> and the <u>tares</u> would mature together and culminate in a great <u>harvest</u>.

E. A generation in Scripture ranges from:

1. Thirty to seventy years.

2. <u>Forty to one hundred years.</u>

3. Thirty to one hundred years.

4. Twenty to eighty years.

Lesson 3: The Signs of the Times

A. Which of the following sign trends in the Church will precede the return of Jesus?

1. <u>The unprecedented evangelization of the earth.</u>

2. The sealing of the Lord's servants, protecting them from persecution.

3. The completing of the Great Commission through the full conversion of all nations.

4 <u>The widespread compromise of the faith by many believers.</u>

B. The book of Revelation tells us that a remnant of believers will come forth from every <u>tribe</u>, <u>tongue</u>, <u>people</u>, and <u>nation</u> before the judgment events of the end times.

C. True—There will be persecution against believers in a manner that will be unique in all of church history.

D. There will be widespread <u>heresy</u> in the Church as many false teachers and prophets emerge at the end of the age, leading to unprecedented <u>apostasy</u>.

E. For the first time in thousands of years, houses of prayer are established in the city of Jerusalem, similar to the prophecy by which Old Testament prophet:

1. Elijah

2. Zechariah

3. Joel

    4.   <u>Isaiah</u>

Lesson 4: Overview of the End Times

A. The <u>Day</u> of the <u>Lord</u> refers to the unusual end-time events related to the second coming of Jesus.

B. Understanding the sequence of events revealed in the book of <u>Daniel</u> is critical to understanding the timing of the end-time events described in the book of Revelation and elsewhere in Scripture.

C. How long will the Great Tribulation last?

    1.   Seven years

    2.   Seventy weeks

    3.   <u>Forty-two months</u>

    4.   <u>A time, times, and half a time</u>

D. During the Great Tribulation, what is not a source of pressure?

    1.   The wrath of God on the rebellious.

    2.   The rage of Satan against the saints.

    3.   <u>The renewal of the earth to an Eden-like paradise.</u>

    4.   The actions of evil people against one another.

E. The rapture of the church will not be a <u>secret</u> event, but a <u>dramatic</u> one witnessed by all believers and unbelievers.

Lesson 5: Introduction to the Book of Revelation

A. Which of the following is the book of Revelation focused on describing?

    1.   The character and personality of Jesus as the Savior, Healer, and Provider.

    2.   God's action plan to remove the earth.

    3.   <u>The role of the Church in partnering with Jesus to release the judgments of God.</u>

    4.   <u>The necessary preparation to endure and overcome in the midst of great trouble.</u>

B. The book of Revelation is a "canonized" <u>prayer</u> <u>manual</u> to prepare the Church for the events of the end times.

C. There is no contradiction between Jesus as <u>Bridegroom</u> and <u>Judge</u>.

D. The three central themes in the book of Revelation are:

1. <u>Kingdom</u>

2. Justification

3. <u>Tribulation</u>

4. <u>Perseverance</u>

E. The book of Revelation describes in detail two <u>global</u> <u>worship</u> movements that will grow to fullness at the end of the age.

Lesson 6: Overview of the Book of Revelation

A. The Father's primary purpose in giving us the book of Revelation is to reveal the <u>beauty</u> of Jesus, and it is secondarily a book about <u>events</u> in the end times.

B. The end-time judgments in the book of Revelation are <u>literal</u> (actual events not to be explained away symbolically), <u>future</u> (their greatest fulfillment is still to come), <u>progressive</u> (increasing in intensity), and <u>numbered</u> (released in sequential order).

C. The book of Revelation contains the following:

1. <u>Four main parts</u>

2. <u>Five chronological sections</u>

3. Four angelic explanations

4. <u>Seven primary symbols</u>

D. The seven seals are released by <u>Jesus</u>.

E. The judgments of Revelation are an end-time application of the Egyptian <u>plagues</u> to prepare the saints for a final <u>exodus</u> from this present evil age to the new kingdom order.

IHOPU
INTERNATIONAL HOUSE OF PRAYER UNIVERSITY
Encounter God. Do His Works. Change the World.

FOUR FULL-TIME SCHOOLS
- MINISTRY SCHOOL
- MUSIC SCHOOL
- MEDIA SCHOOL
- MISSIONS SCHOOL*

International House of Prayer University (IHOPU) is a higher education institution of theology and practical ministry training, grounded in the Word of God.

Our mandate is to equip and send out believers who love Jesus and others wholeheartedly to preach the Word, heal the sick, serve the poor, plant churches, start houses of prayer, and proclaim the return of Jesus.

IHOPU's 1,000 students from 20 countries are part of the International House of Prayer, an evangelical missions organization centered on 24/7 worship-based prayer. It is our joy to see students mature as intercessors, singers, musicians, evangelists, and media messengers, as they engage in wholehearted prayer, outreach, and works of compassion.

Features
- Visas for international students
- Internships for all ages
- Skilled faculty
- Passion for Jesus and compassion for people
- eSchool, training students around the world

* U.S. applicants only

APPLY TODAY

 IHOP.org/ihopu

IHOP.org

816.763.0200 x.3302
eschool@ihop.org
IHOP.org/eschool

IHOPU eSchool serves the IHOPU mandate of equipping individuals, local churches, and houses of prayer throughout the earth. Our eSchool courses bring training you would receive at IHOPU directly to you. IHOPU eSchool courses help students go deep in the Word, develop intimacy with Jesus, grow in the ministry of the Holy Spirit, and love Jesus and others wholeheartedly.

INTERACTIVE COURSES

- Simulate the on-campus IHOPU experience
- High-quality video and audio recordings of lectures, with course notes, tests, and more
- Corporate prayer component
- Online course facilitator
- Online discussion forums
- Option to apply for IHOPU credit

ENRICHMENT COURSES

- Ideal for personal enrichment; no required course assignments
- Choose from audio or video streaming, each with corresponding course notes

GROUP STUDY COURSES

- Designed for home groups, and Bible studies
- Perfect for starting a training center in your church or house of prayer
- DVD-based curriculum, accompanied by notes and exams
- Mailed to your door

SIGNIFICANT DISCOUNTS ON COURSE PACKAGES
IHOP.org/eschool

IHOP–KC Prayer Room Webstream

24/7 Live Worship with Prayer

Join us in the prayer room via our free 24/7 webstream. Whether you are in your dorm room, at home, in your office, or at the gym, you can join us for worship and prayer, day and night.

Many groups use the live webstream to provide worship and intercession for their prayer meetings by projecting life-size images onto a large screen.

We hear numerous testimonies from around the world of people being blessed by the webstream in their private devotions, of the benefit of live worship from the prayer room in homegroups, and even of prisons providing the webstream to inmates.

IHOP.org/prayerroom

MIKEBICKLE.org
FREE Teaching Library

IHOP.org

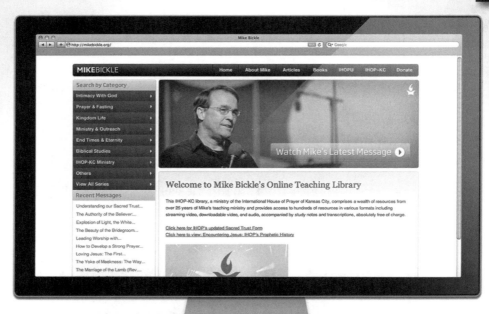

Encompassing more than 25 years of Mike Bickle's teaching ministry, this free, online library from IHOP–KC contains hundreds of messages in multiple formats:

- Video - streaming and download
- Audio - streaming and download
- Teaching notes
- Transcripts

Mike's most requested titles are all here, including series such as *Studies in the Bride of Christ*, *The First Commandment*, *The Book of Revelation*, and *Encountering Jesus*.

MikeBickle.org

internships

Each of our four internships are dedicated to praying for the release of the fullness of God's power and purpose, as interns actively win the lost, heal the sick, feed the poor, and minister in the power of the Holy Spirit. Our vision is to work in relationship with the larger Body of Christ to serve the Great Commission, as we seek to walk out the two great commandments to love God and people. Our desire is to see each intern build strong relationships and lifelong friendships.

INTRO TO IHOP-KC

This program, consisting of two three-month tracks, offers classes about IHOP–KC's values, ministries, and structure, and teaches practical skills for interns to succeed long-term as intercessory missionaries. This internship is for people of all ages, both families and singles.

ONE THING INTERNSHIP

A six-month residential program for single young adults, ages 18–25.

FIRE IN THE NIGHT

A residential program consisting of two three-month tracks for single young adults, ages 18–30. Fire in the Night is part of the IHOP–KC NightWatch and operates on a night schedule.

SIMEON COMPANY

This program consists of two three-month tracks and is for those age 50 and over, whether married or single.

Six months of any internship qualify participants to apply to become IHOP-KC staff.

International House of Prayer University
12901 S. US Highway 71, Grandview, MO 64030
816.763.0200 • internships@ihop.org • IHOP.org/internships